Beyond My Pain: Living Mindfully and Compassionately with Mood Disorders

Bill Lee

©2014 by Bill Lee
All rights reserved. Published 2014
No portion of this publication may be reproduced or transmitted in any form or by any means, electronic or mechanical, including photocopying, recording, or by any information storage and retrieval system, without permission in writing from the author. Thank you for your support.

ISBN-13: 978-1500126360
ISBN-10: 1500126365

http://chineseplayground.com

email: mail@chineseplayground.com

First Paperback Edition: June 2014

Cover design and photo: Bill Lee

Excerpt from *Born to Lose* used with permission from Hazelden Publishing

Author's note: The contents of this book are for informational purposes only. This publication is not intended as a substitute for the advice of health care professionals.

Also by Bill Lee

Chinese Playground: A Memoir

Born to Lose: Memoirs of a Compulsive Gambler

This book is dedicated
to all those who have been
traumatized by violence

Contents

Introduction

Chapter 1. An Unlikely Buddhist

Chapter 2. Mindful Living

Chapter 3. Interconnectedness, Forgiveness, & Compassion

Chapter 4. Psychodrama

Chapter 5. Transactional Analysis and the Inner Adapted Child

Chapter 6. A Dark Life Script

Chapter 7. Buddhism: An Organic Path

Chapter 8. Hiking Meditation

Chapter 9. Embracing Nightmares, Flashbacks, and Ruminations

Chapter 10. Healing My Adapted Child

Chapter 11. Tonglen: The Power of Compassion

Chapter 12. Releasing the Trauma

Chapter 13. Right Speech and Right Living

Chapter 14. Suffering and Addiction

Chapter 15. Attachments

Chapter 16. Toxic Karma: Treating Children as Commodities

Chapter 17. Keeping Things in Perspective: Road Rage and Bird Poop

Chapter 18. Mindful Consumption and Maintenance

Conclusion

Sources, Recommended Readings, and Other Information

Gratitude

About the Author

Excerpt from Chinese Playground

Excerpt from Born to Lose

I'm leaning against the wall in our company cafeteria, dressed in a three-piece suit, becoming increasingly agitated by the minute. My coworkers and I are all gathered at an all-hands meeting, where our divisional vice president is presenting his report on the company's performance for the latest quarter. There's a fellow I don't recognize, standing on the other side of the room directly across from me. I can barely make out his facial features, but I know for certain that he's been "staring me down" as soon as I arrived. What is this guy's problem? Do I know you? I'm too old to be getting into a staring contest with this dude, but I'm not about to let him disrespect me. It's been a good fifteen minutes and he's still at it. Okay, now he's got a smirk on his face, like he thinks he's better than me. As soon as the clapping stops and people start exiting, I make a beeline for the guy. If he's looking for trouble, he found it. As I strut forward, I'm sizing the guy up. He's got at least four inches on me, but his wiry physique and droopy posture indicate a weak core and stance. The dude finally breaks his stare and turns away. Too late, 'cause I am psyched up. He messed with the wrong guy. Just as I get within fifteen feet of him, he turns and faces me. I see the white cane and my entire body freezes. Man, I'm an idiot.

Introduction

I have been in therapy for most of my adult life. I've been treated for depression, anxiety, acute stress, bipolar disorder II, post-traumatic stress, intermittent explosive disorder, OCD (obsessive compulsive disorder), and addiction. Mental illness runs in my family—on both sides—and it goes back at least two generations. I feel fortunate that I have been functional for the majority of my life and I have never been delusional. That's not to make light of mood disorder symptoms, which can be debilitating. I have suffered five severe manic episodes—mental breakdowns, in layman terms. The last occurred in 2003. During those episodes, I was unable to work or care for myself.

The guidance and support from my therapists provided insight into my disorders and helped me to function, but my despair, anxiety, anger, impulsivity, mood swings, cravings, violent flashbacks, and ruminations persisted. My medicine cabinets have been stocked with a variety of psychotropic medications, including antidepressants, mood stabilizers, and anti-anxiety as well as other off-label drugs. None of them offered much to alleviate my symptoms. In fact, a misdiagnosis and titrating of (SSRI) antidepressant medications by several physicians contributed to suicidal ideation and manic episodes over an extended period. The mood stabilizers' sedative effect mellowed me out a bit, but the side effects, including tardive dyskinesia, led me to seriously question the benefit-risk tradeoff.

By the age of eight, I had already exhibited symptoms of manic depression. I was hyper, irritable, easily agitated, had little need for sleep, and was a chronic school truant. I contended with racing thoughts, worried obsessively, and exhibited high-risk, aggressive, and hostile behavior. I got into fistfights almost daily, stole, scaled buildings, climbed rooftops, and played cat-and-mouse with the police like it was a game. I was on edge, twenty-four seven—always expecting the worst to happen. I attribute my personality trait of being a perfectionist to a combination of OCD, from constantly being criticized and ridiculed as a child, and a desperate need to be perfect in order to control my environment. Rarely did I feel physically or emotionally safe—in places or with people—including my own family. I was always anxious, afraid that a fight would break out at any moment. When I encountered someone for the first time, I naturally sized them up as though we were about to engage in combat. When I entered public establishments such as a restaurant, store, or theater, my first order of business was to scrutinize the crowd for enemies and to plan an escape route. In fact, I was interviewed for a magazine article after my first book was published, and when the piece was printed, it contained the following paragraph: *"Bill Lee and I spoke in a small café in March. Although open and detailed in talking about the subject in hand, thirty years after leaving the gang life Lee still seemed alert to an unseen threat, furtively scanning the room before starting our interview and asking me politely not to print the café's location after we were done."* I'm surprised the journalist didn't also mention that I sat strategically facing the entryway, with my back to the wall.

My perception of the world was that it was "dog eat dog," cruel, and unpredictable. I quickly adopted a survival instinct, which relied upon being secretive, cunning, resourceful, and aggressive. It took tremendous effort for anyone to gain my trust, especially since I didn't really trust myself. My core belief was that it was me against the world. At times, I felt like it was *me* against me.

In my previous memoirs, I detailed my upbringing in a violent and emotionally toxic home, hustling in the streets as a child, gambling and seeking sanctuary in violent gangs. Witnessing my mother's suicide attempts, being subjected to my father's drunken rages, and other violence in the home bequeathed me with post-traumatic stress disorder. However, nightmares and flashbacks of those events simply augmented the recurring images of shootings, savage assaults, and grisly crime scenes—remnants of my secret life in the Chinese underworld. When an all-out gang war in San Francisco Chinatown culminated in a restaurant massacre, I was questioned by the police as a person of interest. Twenty years later, fate (or perhaps karma) would lead me to Silicon Valley, where another massacre—this time at my workplace—would shake up my already fragile psyche.

Although I graduated from college with honors, and achieved a so-called "successful" career, my motivation was driven by a constant need for attention and approval because—deep down—I felt worthless and was consumed with self-hatred. I compensated for my insecurities by placing a high value on money, career, and material possessions; and by feeding my inflated ego, criticizing, bullying, and acting out my aggression. When I competed, it was win by any means necessary and at all costs. Working tirelessly and gambling recklessly—nonstop for days at a time—were some of the ways I self-medicated to offset bouts of major depression and to numb my emotional pain. Although my bosses and clients repeatedly labeled me a superstar, they had no idea of my ongoing internal turmoil. If they did, they kept it to themselves.

For most of my life, a perceived dirty look, crossed words, or simple teasing was enough to trigger my anger and propensity for violence. My (positive) coping and conflict-resolution skills were negligible. It was unsettling to wake up each morning, fearing that I might end up in the hospital, morgue, or in jail because I could be so easily provoked and unable to control my rage. To be constantly afraid of oneself is a horrible feeling. Part of the problem was that, although I had physically removed myself from the gang life after college, the gangster inside of me lived on, and the frightened child within still perceived the world as a huge battlefield.

When I shared my dark secrets with therapists, I worried that they would have me committed, or report me to authorities for being a danger to myself or others. One of them was so concerned that at the end of each session, she had me enter a verbal contract with her by reciting and agreeing to the following: *I will not hurt myself or anyone else—on purpose or by accident—no matter what happens.* It worked for a good period of time. Eventually, I switched therapists and, at my suggestion, we continued utilizing the verbal contract. When she abruptly ended our relationship for reasons unbeknownst to me, all bets were off.

My son kept me out of a lot of trouble. His mother and I shared custody of him since he was eighteen months old and his presence had a calming effect on me. Not wanting my child to turn out like me was a great motivator for me to be on my best behavior around him.

*M*y interest in Buddhism and eastern philosophy began as a pip-squeak Kung-Fu film buff with a penchant for sneaking into neighborhood movie houses. I was enthralled by the Shaolin monks up on the screen displaying amazing feats, while calmly extolling Buddhist and Taoist virtues of compassion, humility, and morality. In my early teens, I was indoctrinated to meditation and breathing techniques to cultivate *chi* as part of my martial arts training. Throughout my life, when I sought personal growth or faced emotional crises—in addition to therapy—eastern philosophy was the source I turned to for insight and guidance.

In 2003, when I was consumed with thoughts of suicide, Pema Chödrön's book, *When Things Fall Apart: Heart Advice for Difficult Times*, provided a lifeline. For example, I found the practice of embracing suffering (*dukkha* in Pali) more empowering than attempting to suppress it or turning it over (to a higher power). The concept of viewing our enemies as "gurus," who can teach us valuable lessons was enlightening as well. My interest in Buddhism was piqued once again, but my practice was short-lived as I lacked the mental discipline and moral fiber to abide by the precepts or to dedicate myself to the Four Noble Truths, which are the essence of the Buddha's teachings on suffering. My emotions were simply too fragile at the time. However, I began practicing mindfulness (*sati* in Pali) sitting meditation as a coping mechanism to deal with gambling urges. It was frustrating in the beginning; I didn't realize how little control I had of my mind. I had a difficult time shutting off my thoughts. Any progress I made came with a price. For example, as I focused and let go of mundane thoughts, negative images from my past would emerge. I kept at it, but I didn't realize the full benefits of mindfulness until years later, when two things occurred: I started hiking; and I embraced Buddhism.

There are many ways to practice mindfulness, which is the seventh element of the Eightfold Path of Buddhism. Some train by temporarily deactivating all five senses as well as the mind, while others utilize techniques that rely *on* the senses. I believe that, while practicing mindfulness is difficult for most people, it poses additional challenges for those individuals who suffer from recurring nightmares, flashbacks, and ruminations—symptoms of PTSD. At the same time, I can attest that mindfulness can be a formidable tool for treating this disorder.

In 2009, I started power hiking for the cardio benefits. After just a few outings, I experienced periods of calmness and clarity. This motivated me to delve into walking meditation (known in Zen Buddhism as *kinhin*), since I wasn't able to locate any books on hiking meditation. This led to a renewed interest and commitment to the Buddhist tradition. I applied what I learned to hiking, adding my own techniques along the way. After a few months, I discovered that mindful hiking and the teachings of Buddhism—when combined with my experience in psychotherapy—benefited my mood disorders. Adopting this lifestyle, which I refer to as *magga* (Pali word meaning a path to the cessation of suffering) has transformed my life, leading me to be more calm, relaxed, patient, compassionate, and virtuous. It awakened me to my *inner Buddha* (true nature; enlightened self), which is pure, peaceful, kind, compassionate, nurturing, and non-judgmental. This path has empowered me to comfort and heal many of my psychic wounds. My mood is more stable, I have firmer control of my thoughts and emotions, I sleep better, I experience less anxiety, and I have added a powerful coping mechanism. The frequencies of my nightmares, flashbacks, and ruminations have lessened considerably—some have ceased altogether. Instead of repressing or running away from them, I embrace each one as they appear, study them, make friends with each one—then release them.

Throughout this book, I describe the crucial role that compassion plays in my magga. I also detail some of the insights and emotional breakthroughs I have experienced. Virtually all of them occurred on the hiking trails. This doesn't mean others can't reap the same benefits from practicing other forms of meditation (both movement and non-movement) and mindfulness. I just happened to discover that it's easier for me to release my thoughts and focus while I'm hiking on quiet, scenic trails.

My bipolar disorder is in remission, based on established psychiatric diagnostic criteria. When my psychiatrist informed me of this, I didn't exactly jump up and down. Indifferent would be a more accurate and appropriate description of my response. In the following pages, readers will come to understand why.

This is not intended to be a how-to book. My hope is that by sharing my experiences, it will motivate others affected by mental illness to learn more about how the integration of mindfulness meditation, psychotherapy, and a spiritual practice could be beneficial for them or someone they love. At the very least, I think readers will gain insight into the cause and effect of one man's dark view of himself and the world. Conceptual words in their native text (mostly Pali and Sanskrit) are included so readers can learn more about their origin and alternate interpretations—doing so also pays homage to their respective traditions. In kindness and with gratitude, I share my humble journey with you.

Chapter 1
An Unlikely Buddhist

*B*uddhism cultivates calmness, loving-kindness, compassion, mindfulness, selflessness, non-attachment, and ethical behavior. I, on the other hand, have lived the majority of my life in the complete opposite manner. So how did someone like me, after numerous attempts, finally come to embrace this tradition? My discovery of mindfulness played a big part, while the 12-Step Recovery Program deserves some credit as well. For fifteen years, I was an active member in Gamblers Anonymous. Buddhism and 12-Step fellowships have a lot in common. Both traditions promote community (*sangha*), spirituality, humility, accountability, making amends, ethical behavior, and of course—abstinence from intoxicants. In fact, when I review all my notes from doing Step work over a period of ten years, the goals I outlined, coincidentally, are in accordance with the Eightfold Path. One major difference between 12-Step fellowships and Buddhism is that the former advocate surrendering to a higher power, while the latter emphasizes the power within each of us.

I battled gambling addiction for forty years and came close to self-destructing. At my lowest point, I believed that the only way to halt my gambling was to kill the *host body*. Yet, it was my active participation in Gamblers Anonymous that led to my transformation. Through the program, I developed positive coping strategies, matured emotionally, learned humility, and worked on my character defects. I reconnected with my spirituality and allowed myself to be vulnerable. By reaching out and supporting fellow addicts, I was able to relate to others with kindness, acceptance, and compassion. In working the Steps, I took responsibility for my actions—both past and present. In time, I felt better about myself and started to believe that, beneath the "emotional Kevlar," I was a good person who *deserved* recover*y*. All of this planted the seed for me to train in mindfulness, which helped me to develop the discipline and concentration necessary to practice Buddhism.

Chapter 2

Mindful Living

*M*indful living is simply being fully in the here and now. For someone like me, who has been haunted by my past and worried incessantly about the future, being present helps me to maintain a calm, disciplined mind. Mindfulness meditation liberates me from obsessive worrying, so I'm able to function fully in the moment. This doesn't mean I never reflect on previous events or avoid making plans. It just means that this is done at my discretion, in a focused, astute manner. It's like having an orchestra conductor inside my mind, who also serves as a gatekeeper. When I'm free of discursive thoughts, I can concentrate, reach a higher consciousness, and embrace insights, which have resulted in emotional breakthroughs and healing. Practicing mindfulness keeps me accountable for my speech and actions. It also serves as a potent, healthy coping mechanism. When I'm in a stressful situation or find myself becoming anxious or hyper, I immediately implement mindful breathing, instead of panicking, acting out angrily, or resorting to old habits—such as self-medicating. It brings my mind to a restful state where it can stabilize and recharge, while maintaining full awareness. (Breathing and awareness are both functions of the brain stem.) Mindfulness meditation strengthens my focus and concentration, and helps me to gain deeper insight into both my conscious and unconscious mind (referenced in Buddhism as *alaya* or *stored consciousness*). These attributes are essential in my spiritual practice.

Early on in my mindfulness training, I often began meditation sessions feeling like my mind was already calm. I'd set aside ten or fifteen minutes, assuming that the allotted time would be sufficient. However, soon after I began my meditation, worries, concerns, and unresolved issues that had been repressed—lying just below my unconscious mind—would surface. Many times, it would take me up to an hour to address these disturbing thoughts. I learned that the perceived calmness was actually masking my stress and anxiety. I have stopped making assumptions about my mood. I do my best to allow ample time for my meditation sessions and to use mindfulness—not only to assess my true state of mind—but also to gain better control of it.

Mindfulness reminds me a lot of martial arts, specifically the emphases on mental discipline, alertness, and breathing. Plus, there are no shortcuts; the progress I make and the benefits I reap are proportionate to the amount of dedication and effort I put in. This is the reason I use words such as "exercise" and "training" to describe my practice.

I start each day when I wake up by breathing mindfully for a few minutes while still lying in bed. In addition to my daily hiking, walking, and sitting meditation sessions, I practice spontaneous mindfulness throughout the day by taking frequent, momentary "timeouts" (especially when I experience negative thoughts) that can be as short as three belly breaths (diaphragmatic breathing).

Chapter 3

Interconnectedness, Forgiveness and Compassion

*B*uddhist Zen Master Thich Nhat Hanh (often called "Thay," which means "teacher" in Vietnamese) coined the term "interbeing," highlighting the Buddhist principle of interconnectedness—the concept that all beings are interrelated. He has also referenced the inner child in his teachings. Thay advocates transforming anger into compassion, the latter being the key to forgiveness. He believes this can be practiced by acknowledging that our enemies also suffer. As detailed later in this book, Thay's teachings inspired me to approach my anger, post-traumatic stress and ruminations in a totally radical (for me, anyway) manner.

The practice of forgiveness (*khamanasila* in Pali) is a core component of Buddhism, promoting *metta* (loving kindness) and *karuna* (compassion) toward oneself and others. Yet, this principle has eluded me for most of my life.

I grew up in an environment where forgiveness and compassion were all considered signs of weakness. Being compassionate meant you were soft and a potential liability—someone who could not be trusted. It would be unhealthy to express compassion for adversaries or innocent victims. It meant you might pause momentarily, have second thoughts, or not follow through during a fight or commission of a crime. Even showing compassion for a friend can be misconstrued as pity or disrespect, leading to serious repercussions.

In relation to forgiveness, in my (former) world, if someone harmed you in any way and you did not retaliate, it would invite others to target you as well. Personally, an "eye for an eye" didn't satisfy me. Often, out of anger—which escalated to rage—I wanted the other person to suffer more. The few times that I turned the other cheek and walked away, I berated myself for not *manning up*, believing that I had allowed the person or persons to "punk" me. My insecurities, in the form of needing to "save face," prevented me from rising above it. But this mindset only led to more conflicts, fueling my anxiety, anger, nightmares, and ruminations. These episodes often resulted in hypomania or outright mania, which rapidly cycled down to a depressive crash following the altercations. In time, I would learn from the *Dharma* (teachings of Buddhism) that forgiveness through compassion can be a source of empowerment for someone like me—specifically when I integrate it with mindfulness, along with my past psychotherapy training and treatment.

Chapter 4

Psychodrama

I majored in psychology in college. There was definitely an underlying desire to unravel the trauma and crises I experienced, both at home and in the streets. I'm sure many therapists make a career in the psychotherapeutic field for similar reasons; it's just safer to analyze other people's families. At the time, I convinced myself that my motive was to help others.

After receiving my undergraduate degree, I worked in community mental health and received additional training in various modalities of counseling. Psychodrama therapy, for example, was taught in both didactic and experiential formats. Essentially, attendees (which included experienced therapists) learned and practiced on each other. I recall volunteering and being directed to role-play and have a dialogue with an empty chair that represented a family member, expressing feelings that I had been repressing. Many of the therapists who treated me in the '70s and '80s used psychodrama in our sessions, as it was quite popular at the time. On several occasions, at my therapists' urging, I acted out scenes where I forgave specific people who harmed me. But when I spoke the words, it was disingenuous. On the other hand, expressing my anger, filled with profanities felt liberating. There was some relief following my rants, but it was brief. In hindsight, I was merely applying a band-aid to deep, emotional wounds. My past traumas remained unresolved.

The practices of compassion and forgiveness were foreign concepts to me at the time and would remain so for many decades. After embracing Buddhism, I instinctively integrated psychodrama with the Dharma and mindfulness to treat and heal my suffering.

Chapter 5

Transactional Analysis and the Inner Adapted Child

*O*ne form of psychology and psychotherapy that I became particularly interested in was Transactional Analysis (TA). TA was developed in the 1950s by the late Eric Berne, whose background was in psychoanalysis. I immersed myself in TA after college and became an active, clinical member of a seminar group that included a number of TA pioneers (Steve Karpman, Jack Dusay, Pat Crossman, and Pam Levin) and enthusiasts who met weekly in San Francisco. TA's main theory is that human personality is made up of three ego states: Inner Parent (comprised of *critical* and *nurturing* characteristics); Adult (which is rational and analytical); and Inner Child (made up of the Free Child and the Adapted Child). The Inner Free Child is free-spirited, carefree, trusting, spontaneous, uninhibited, playful, and unencumbered, while the

Inner Adapted Child has learned to survive by either complying or rebelling. The Inner Adapted Child can be very charming, resourceful, cunning and manipulative. For most of my life, my Inner Child functioned primarily in the Adapted Child ego state, which explains my volatile and defiant behavior. (For the remainder of this book, Inner Adapted Child and Inner Nurturing Parent will simply be referred to as Adapted child and Nurturing Parent, respectively.)

One of the most intense programs I ever completed was a week-long, TA-based workshop on self-parenting. About a dozen other participants and I identified what we lacked from our parents, and learned positive self-parenting techniques to support our Inner Child. What I took away from the workshop would be particularly useful many years later in the care and treatment of my mood disorders.

I have spent the majority of my adult life in psychotherapy attempting to understand and heal my Inner Child—specifically, my Adapted Child. In addition to established modes of therapy to treat my mood disorders, I also explored unconventional practices such as hypnosis and EMDR (eye movement desensitization and reprocessing); any benefits gained were temporary. Integrating psychotherapy with mindfulness meditation and the Dharma was not something that I planned; it evolved naturally after I embraced Buddhism.

Chapter 6

A Dark Life Script

Life scripting is a Transactional Analysis theory, which postulates the concept that our life plans are mapped out at an early age, as a result of our observations and interactions with our family, especially our parents. While scripting delineates both positive and negative outcomes, the therapeutic focus has been on assessing and treating individuals with maladjusted and self-destructive patterns. For example, women and men who are repeatedly attracted to romantic partners who are alcoholics or abusive may be playing out their life scripts based on their own family dynamics. As adults, they may unconsciously recast themselves over and over again in the role of a codependent or battered spouse. In the psychotherapeutic field, there are clinicians who are critical of scripting, viewing it as overly simplistic. I believe that the theory has merit, based on my own life and observation of others. I have always been curious about people and their upbringing. I have heard thousands of stories from recovering addicts, who shared intimate details about their childhoods. Plus, I have spent my career interviewing folks from all walks of life, and observed how employees communicate and work with one another. In many situations, I strongly suspected that the friction between colleagues and dysfunction in organizations were re-enactments of drama from the respective employees' childhoods.

Psychotherapist and author Claude Steiner, one of Berne's protégés, is a recognized expert on life scripts. His books include *Scripts People Live* and *The Warm Fuzzy Tale* (he coined the phrase "warm and fuzzy"). I have been intrigued by Steiner's concept of *tragic* life plans, since I first read about it in a college psychology class.

Examining life plans with tragic themes was a rude awakening for me. Even before I was able to put a label on it, I recognized that the neighborhood playground served as a sanctuary for me. It allowed me to escape the turmoil in my home. I just didn't realize that the conflicts and physical violence behind closed doors were so common in my life that, eventually, I sought it out unconsciously. It influenced my perception of how people socialize and resolve their differences. As a result, I bonded with other violent, latchkey kids at the playground and we were the ones who ended up in hardcore gangs. Soon after, I decided that bullying, violence, and committing crimes were realities of life and it was survival of the fittest. People who truly know me will tell you that, for the most part, arguments and confrontations terrify me. Fighting was a means of survival in my mind and one of the storylines I played out from a script that was formulated in my childhood home.

Unwanted and a Burden

I described in my previous books how—when my mother became pregnant with me—my parents attempted to medically abort me (more on this later). Following my birth, my parents entered into negotiations to sell me to a childless couple. When I became deadly ill at age four, the deal fell apart. I was considered damaged goods, presumably, so I remained with my biological family. Nevertheless, my parents constantly told me that I was a burden: my mother when she was stressed out, which happened often; and my dad when he was drunk—a nightly ritual.

Sadly, children do not have the capacity to filter, buffer, or rationalize their parents' toxic behavior. It was beyond my scope to reassure myself that my father and mother did not really mean those nasty remarks or that they were hounded by their own demons. I think it's safe to say that their ill-fated attempts to abort and to sell me contributed to my sense of worthlessness, which subsequently manifested in my hostile behavior when I felt that I was being judged, criticized, disrespected, or rejected. Throughout my lifetime, I have become acquainted with other people who were also plagued with deep-rooted self-esteem issues. Their parents may not have attempted to physically get rid of them, but there are other ways that parents emotionally abandon their children, or cause them to believe that they're a burden. Some fellow victims I met acted out catastrophic life scripts where they directed their anger inward by numbing themselves with intoxicants or physically hurting themselves, while others reacted violently in response to a perceived dirty look or rejection—as though their existence was being questioned, disregarded, or threatened.

Before studying psychology, I already figured out that most of my delinquent behavior growing up was a cry for attention. I wasn't secure enough to ask for a hug as a child, or to articulate that I was in deep, emotional pain, so I sought negative attention. In my mind, negative validation was better than none at all. Later, while learning about life scripts, I thought about my middle school homeroom teacher, Mr. S., whom I had terrorized. I constantly disrupted his class and mocked him, eventually pushing him beyond his boiling point. One day, after the bell rang and all my fellow classmates had exited the classroom, he marched toward me in the corner, where I had been ordered to stand facing the wall. As Mr. S. began lecturing me again, I started laughing and waved him off. Suddenly, he screamed, "William, you will never amount to anything and will just end up in jail!" This remark predicting what my future holds would be replayed in my head over and over for many years. The fact that I didn't immediately attack him or plan some elaborate retaliation surprised me. After studying TA scripts, it occurred to me that I wasn't merely seeking negative attention from Mr. S., but egging him to deem that I was a burden in order to reaffirm my self-perception and life plan. His out-of-character declaration was my "payoff." Mr. S. wasn't the first—and he would not be the last—authority figure that I cast in my real-life dramas. My Buddhist practice now includes ongoing prayers for each of them (or their spirits).

*W*hen I graduated from college, I fooled myself into believing that by leaving the gang life, I was rewriting my life plan. But I still perceived the world as a battlefield and merely switched stages. Upon hearing about the competitive business landscape in Silicon Valley, my antennae went up and that's where I focused my career. Unconsciously, I enlisted in corporate warfare with numerous high tech firms in the South Bay, where I would serve as a "soldier" (headhunter) and eventually a "hired gun" (independent consultant) for the next thirty years—operating under the mandate of "business is war," "take no prisoners," and "win at all costs." My services included establishing war libraries and spying on competitors. In both my personal and professional life, I continued my penchant for conflict, often picking fights with people, especially individuals who reminded me of my family and childhood enemies. I would continue on this dark path until my last relapse forced me to take complete inventory of my life. It wasn't until I committed to Buddhism and my magga that I liberated myself from my destructive script.

I have created a lot of havoc and caused considerable harm to others in my lifetime—beginning when I first set foot onto the playground as a frightened and angry little boy—up until I became a Buddhist. Perhaps karma is behind all the pain, suffering, and trauma I have endured in my lifetime, affirming the concept that "what goes around comes around." I learned the hard way that in order for me to awaken my heart and mind, my path must begin with the cultivation of compassion for myself. I cannot be kind to others unless I nurture myself first.

Chapter 7

Buddhism: An Organic Path

*V*irtually all of the therapists who treated me over the years used a rational approach involving talk therapy. Psychodynamic and CBT (cognitive behavior therapies) were the primary modalities employed. Issues were identified and action plans were developed and implemented, followed by monitoring and measurement of any progress; in essence, a linear model. Treatment plans typically stipulated, upfront, a specific number of sessions, which were nearly always dictated by the terms of the health coverage policy I happened to be enrolled in at the time. Otherwise, it was an out-of-pocket expense, which really shortened the treatment plan. Reflecting back on it now, I see that these sessions generated a large amount of insightful information, which I confused with progress and healing. The data was absorbed by my Adult ego state, yet my symptoms and suffering persisted.

It goes without saying that knowledge is a powerful resource that can impel positive changes. I have friends who either read a book or viewed a film about how food is manufactured and that, alone, motivated them to become vegetarians or vegans. In the same vein, there are millions of people who have attended classes or informational seminars and what they learned inspired them to start businesses or plan for retirement. Conversely, I have met thousands of recovering addicts who admit they have a disease and seek help wholeheartedly. These men and women regularly attend 12-Step meetings, absorb the literature, work with a sponsor, and articulately verbalize what they need to do for their recovery. Yet, most of them continue to struggle and relapse. My point is that while information is an invaluable tool, emotional healing also needs to touch, nurture, and empower the Inner Child, specifically the Adapted Child.

As my past experience in therapy utilized a rational approach, my Buddhist practice is what I would consider an organic path. By this, I mean that Buddhism advocates healing to occur naturally—without a timeline. It is based on the concept that all living organisms are interconnected and that, deep down, we are pure and good; it's a matter of discovering it. Insight and knowledge are just part of the equation. The Dharma offers many ways for me to empower my Adapted Child.

Chapter 8

Hiking Meditation

When I started hiking, meditating at the same time never entered my mind. It didn't seem possible. Now I practice mindful hiking and walking on a daily basis. It has become a vital part of my life—just as important as food, water, air, and sleep. And this is coming from someone who used to regard walking as utterly boring.

I find it easier to be present when I'm on-the-go, outdoors—as opposed to sitting meditation. I can focus on my breath (belly breathing), concentrate (non-discursive thoughts), and embrace any insights. My favorite trails are quite steep and unpaved, so it's imperative that I look ahead at the ground and plan my steps.

When I first started hiking, having to focus on the ground kept me in the present moment. Still, it was challenging. I would tell myself to focus either on an object in front of me, my steps, or breathing, but after just a few seconds, other thoughts would occupy my mind. So I would pick out a bush or tree about twenty-five yards away and challenge myself to stay present until I reached it. Yet, by the time I hit my mark, I realized that within that short interval, my mind had wandered off and was filled with discursive thoughts such as grocery shopping, what I'm having for lunch, or a film I recently watched. I gave up on a few occasions, but within a day or two, I would train again after reassuring myself that it would take time, practice, and most of all—patience. I started back at square one and chose bushes and trees merely a few yards away and extended the distances in small increments. In time, I got better at staying focused and utilizing my breathing. Alternatively, I counted the number of steps I took in rhythm with my *in* and *out* breaths, noting the changes that occurred when the terrain of the trails shifted. Eventually, I developed additional techniques to remain (or return to being) present. This made a huge difference in my progress, while enhancing both my hiking and walking experiences.

Mindful Breathing, Sketching, and Listening

*I*n the mid-1980s, I enrolled in a holistic vision improvement course. In it, students were taught a technique whereby we pretended to have a pencil attached to our nose. The objective was to sketch surrounding objects, in order to discourage staring and to keep our heads, necks, and shoulders limber. So when I started hiking and walking on a regular basis and wanted to take a break from focusing on my breathing, I improvised what I learned earlier in the vision class by visualizing a foot-long artist paintbrush attached to my nose. It was an experiment, yet I found that sketching was a great way to be (and remain) present. Both activities stimulate the right brain, so they complement each other.

Initially, I sketched the contours of pebbles, rocks, debris, crevices—even shadows on the ground—in front of me. Then, when my path was clear and it was *safe* to look away, I moved on to plants, trees, insects, birds, deer, hills as well as mountain tops, clouds, and so on. When I'm walking in the city, objects such as mailboxes, parking meters, power lines, manhole covers, vehicle license plates, dogs, and people keep my nose brush active. One advantage of having an imaginary nose brush is that one can be creative with it. Mine can be extended and retracted at will, so I reach out and stroke things with the tip—such as petals of a flower, the contour of leaves, or a squirrel climbing up in a tree.

On my walks and hikes, I alternate from focusing on my breathing and sketching to utilizing sounds as another technique to practice mindfulness. For example: birds chirping, insects buzzing, leaves rustling, winds gusting, rain falling—even the sound each time my shoes make contact with the ground. The key is to focus on each breath, sketch, or sound—fully in the moment—then move on. It took time for me to overcome distractions, such as wondering what the tiny birds were cheeping about or where a squirrel was headed.

In the beginning of my mindfulness training, I was still overly sensitive and self-conscious. During my hikes, when I heard the loud tweets of birds, my reaction was, *Hey, they're mocking me*. Now I sketch them and interpret their sounds as friendly greetings and motivational cheers.

Chapter 9

Embracing Nightmares, Flashbacks and Ruminations

*M*y initial interest in mindful hiking was to maintain my exercise regimen while cultivating calmness and clarity. Through the practice of Buddhism, I wanted to be more at peace—with others as well with myself; this entailed abiding by the precepts to the best of my ability and committing to a path of wisdom, ethical conduct (motivated by love and compassion), and mental discipline. I had no expectations that any of this would have a major impact on the symptoms or manifestations of my mood disorders. I did notice that the time I spent on the hiking trails provided me with a respite from the recurring flashbacks and ruminations that have plagued me since I was a small boy. This motivated me to add more hikes to my workout schedule. Then my mindfulness practice took a sharp turn and familiar negative thoughts and images began emerging during my hikes. The difference was that they did not feel intrusive, so I accepted it as a positive development.

Flashes and Flashbacks

*M*y post-traumatic stress disorder results from the trauma and violence I experienced both at home and in the streets, especially during my involvement in the gang wars throughout the '60s and '70s in San Francisco Chinatown. My PTSD manifests in my dreams at night and in flashbacks during the day. Most times, I am reliving the traumatic events. On other occasions, I am observing myself from the sidelines, stepping in and out of the scenes. Often, I just get flashes of people's faces, crime scenes, and bullet-ridden corpses; or get startled by the recurring sounds of punches, kicks, screams, objects breaking, explosions, and gunfire. Conflicts will trigger them, along with viewing violent content on television and in films—or simply hearing familiar music from that era. Ongoing stress increases their frequency. They can also occur without any provocation. (When I work with incarcerated teens, many of whom are hardcore gang members, I share my experiences, highlighting my PTSD as a cautionary tale.)

First Breakthrough

*I*t began as a typical morning on the trail, approximately one month after I began mindful hiking. I had made a personal commitment to the practice of Buddhism and for the past week I had been contemplating Thich Nhat Hanh's teachings on interbeing, compassion, and forgiveness. By now, I had become proficient at being fully present for a good portion of each hike. At that particular moment, I was feeling serene and my mind was void of any thoughts or worries. Buddhists regard this as a higher level of consciousness.

Suddenly, I had a flash. It was the familiar image of a person who attacked me with a mallet when I was fifteen. He was a rival gang member, around my age. For many years, I couldn't get over the trauma and had suffered recurring nightmares, flashbacks, and ruminations of the assault and aftermath. I dealt with this incident repeatedly in therapy, role-playing my dialogue with Johnny (the perpetrator), unleashing my anger at him. As I stated previously, these psychodrama exercises only provided short-term relief for me, if any at all. The umpteen hours spent discussing the beating and aftermath had not brought any closure; only the realization that the repeated blows to my head and face could have killed me.

I was taken aback, but remained calm. My initial reaction was to concentrate and get my focus back to the present moment. But my mindfulness practice kept me relaxed and receptive to what was happening.

For the first time since the incident, I wasn't anxious about Johnny. I saw him as someone who wasn't that different from me—at one time also a frightened, abused little boy—who sought sanctuary in gangs. Then I thought about my role in the dispute that preceded the attack. While maintaining the pace of my hike, I spoke to Johnny, who was holding the mallet. In a gentle manner, I said, *Johnny, I forgive you…and I wish you peace.* I repeated it five or six times. After a short pause, I said to myself, *You're here now…you're on this hill…you are safe now*, repeating this five or half-a-dozen times as well. For the remainder of the hike and throughout the evening, I digested the experience. I didn't know what to make of it at the time, but I felt good about relating to Johnny differently.

The next day, approximately forty-five minutes into my hike, I had an aha moment. It became clear to me that when I spoke to Johnny less than twenty-four hours ago, it was my Adapted Child reaching out to *his* Adapted Child, followed by my Nurturing Parent providing reassurance. I also realized that I had applied Thay's teachings by recognizing the common bond between Johnny and me, and by relating to him with compassion instead of anger—which allowed forgiveness to formulate. I would come to acknowledge this realization as mindfulness insight.

The next flash from the past I experienced on my hike was another image from one of my nightmares. The horrific event involves my mother and father that I have struggled to come to terms with for over forty years. I learned of this secret in my early teens. The scene is one that took place before I was born, so the image was created based on my early memories of their toxic relationship. In it, my parents are having an intense discussion. My mom is pregnant with me and a decision has been made to medically abort. My mother is sitting by a table crying hysterically while my father, who practiced traditional Chinese medicine, is standing over her holding a chipped porcelain rice bowl containing a mixture of herbs he meticulously concocted. She raises the bowl to her lips, jerks her head back and gulps down the lethal potion in one motion.

Part of me understood their reasoning for attempting the abortion, which obviously failed, resulting in my birth with major defects. They were barely able to feed my four older siblings, not to mention support the five children from my father's previous marriages, who were scattered in three different continents. *But how does one get over the fact that their parents essentially tried to end their life?* Whenever I thought about it, I felt both angry and sad, but being furious was easier for me. A disagreement with either one of my parents was all it took to trigger this recurring nightmare. I'd wake up crying, spewing profanities, and screaming, *You never wanted me!*

As a mother deer and her two fawns dashed across and away from me, I suddenly sensed how terrified my parents must have been. I felt sorrow. For once, I understood that it was probably the most difficult decision they ever had to make in their tumultuous marriage. They were afraid that they wouldn't be able to feed and provide adequately for me. My mother may have doubted her fitness as a parent. It also dawned on me that, following my birth, all the congenital defects I had to live with—subsequently requiring surgeries—must have weighed heavily on each of them. I knew that my mother blamed my father for the botched abortion, so they did not lean on one another for support. They suffered alone. The guilt they bore each time I was hospitalized must have been excruciating. *Mommy…Daddy … I'm sorry you suffered so much…and I forgive you.* I repeated the last part to myself three times.

Over the following three months, I relived other past traumatic events. I did my best to respond with compassion, forgiveness, and insight. I was winging it. They typically emerged thirty to forty-five minutes into my hike—seldom more than one per session. This was baffling to me at first. It seemed as though my inner Buddha knew how much I could process at a time. In time, I learned to differentiate between random, discursive thoughts as opposed to flashes and images that were opportunities for insight, breakthroughs, and healing. In the past, these visuals caused tremendous anxiety. With the practice of Buddhism and mindful hiking, I was able to embrace them. I did not attempt to suppress or draw them out. I merely focused on being fully present on the trails. Following are some examples:

Mother's Suicide Attempts

*A*s a young child, I witnessed my mother's multiple suicide attempts in our tiny Chinatown apartment. The images of her in the bathroom swallowing pills, slashing her wrists; and opening the window to jump out—were seared in my brain. The visuals of my siblings and I intervening time and time again are just as traumatic.

As I looked up ahead at the long stretch of steep trail, I suddenly saw myself as a little boy grabbing hold of the hem of my mother's homemade house dress as her torso is partially hanging out the window. Growing up, I was embarrassed by her emotional breakdowns and resented her for being mentally unstable.

I take a deep belly breath and began to tell my mother that I forgave her. But then I thought about the period when I wanted to end my own life, which enabled me to empathize with her feelings of hopelessness and unbearable pain. So instead, I said, *Mommy, now I understand your suffering. Your illness isn't your fault.* Next, my Nurturing Parent spoke to my Adapted Child, who witnessed the horror. *You don't need to be scared. Now you're a strong, loving person. Breathe...focus on the present. You're on this hill at this moment. It's beautiful here. You're safe now. I will protect you. You're safe now. I will protect you. You're safe now. I will protect you.*

First Shooting

*A*s I stopped to take a sip from my water bottle at the bottom of the trail, I suddenly see myself as a small child at a street carnival, where I witnessed my first shooting. I was eight years old. Feuding black and Chinese gangs had agreed to rumble in an alleyway during a street carnival. When it went down, I was standing up front and center with the blacks to my left and our guys on my right. After seeing clubs, pipes, chains, belts, and knives being whipped out, I noticed two dudes from our side tussling over something. It looked to me like they were tucking at each other's belts. Suddenly a loud pop rang out. A split second later, I saw a puff of smoke rising above as one of them fell forward. Someone screamed, "GUN!" and all hell broke loose. I was on my own and was nearly trampled, but somehow made it back home. Although only one shot was fired, POP…POP…POP kept going off in my head. I suddenly attained the ability to distinguish between the sound of exploding firecrackers and gunfire. I found out the following day at the playground that the two guys I saw struggling were brothers. One had tried to stop the other from pulling out a gun and was accidentally shot.

Over the next two decades, I would witness many other casualties of street gang warfare, much more gruesome than the first one. Each incident would be recorded in my memory bank and replayed in my dreams. Most of my therapists held my parents accountable for leaving me unsupervised, but I always defended them. Like so many other immigrants, I knew they both worked hard to put food on the table. I blamed myself for being attracted to gangs and for being a troublemaker.

As I took my first step back up the hill, it came to me—one of those mindfulness aha moments. I realized that beginning as a young boy, I subconsciously weighed the pros and cons of spending time at home versus being out on the streets. There was a lot of violence, vices, and weirdoes in the neighborhood, but in our home, I felt less safe—both physically and emotionally. So I chose what was, in my mind, the lesser of two evils; the risk of getting shot was preferred over the possibility of seeing my mother kill herself. The excitement that came from participating in gangs was also how I self-medicated, to numb my inner pain. Again, my Nurturing Parent reassured my Adapted Child:

You don't need to beat yourself up. You didn't feel safe at home. Breathe…focus on the present. You're on this hill hiking at this very moment. You don't need to run away. It's beautiful here. You're safe now. You don't need violence in your life. I will protect you. You're safe now. I will protect you. You're safe now. I will protect you.

Workplace Massacre

"Good morning." I looked up and was taken aback.

"Uh…yes, it is," I replied politely. The woman, who was using walking poles, traversed past me in the opposite direction as I avoided eye contact and continued my descent. She had no idea that our little encounter instantly brought me back to February 16, 1988 and the massacre at my workplace. This fellow hiker could have passed as a twin of the woman who charged at me and grabbed my lapels that fateful Tuesday. My frustrated, grief-stricken (but harmless) assailant had correctly sensed that I was withholding information regarding her ex-husband, a coworker of mine who had been fatally wounded earlier in the afternoon. But I was instructed to keep mum as we were awaiting confirmation from the coroner.

Twenty-five years have passed and the building where the rampage took place is no longer standing, but that hasn't stopped me from continually reliving it: hearing the gunshots; escorting my visitor out of the building; rushing back in to evacuate my coworkers; working with the police and counselors throughout the five-hour standoff; supporting grieving victims' families during and after the tragedy. One of the bullets fired by Farley, the gunman, ricocheted directly in front of my office. Although he and I never met face-to-face, the image of him aiming and firing his rifle while chasing me has fueled my nightmares on many nights. But more disturbing are the anguished faces of the deceased victims' loved ones that I interacted with. For over twenty years, I had been anxiously awaiting the state of California to carry out Farley's execution at San Quentin State Prison, believing that it would relieve some of my suffering. But I have since had a change of heart, which was initiated by my encounter with the poled hiker.

The picture in my head of my murdered coworker's ex-wife naturally made me think of Farley. Then, as I continued my descent down the hill, while still in a mindful state, I focused on understanding what compelled Farley that horrific day, armed with an arsenal of rifles, handguns, and over a thousand rounds of ammo. He was fired for stalking a coworker over a four-year period. She had rejected his romantic overtures. Most of us have experienced the devastation of being rejected—by someone or something we hold dear. Unrequited love, a breakup, death of a loved one, and job loss are some of the life events that test our resolve and cause individuals to snap. These letdowns can reinforce deep-rooted self-perceived notions, such as failure, helplessness, abandonment, and worthlessness.

As I turn away from the sun and exhale fully, I imagine Farley as a socially awkward little boy, constantly teased and unable to fend for himself. Although I cannot fathom targeting strangers and innocent bystanders, I have felt rage in the past, to the point of wanting to shoot individuals who had harmed me or people I cared about.

I forgive you, Richard Farley. I forgive you for the trauma I suffered. I cannot forgive you for the other people you killed or injured. That's between you, them, and their families. I do forgive you for what I went through. I forgive you for shooting toward my office. I forgive you. I forgive you. I forgive you.

Ruminations

I have contended with ruminations as far back as I can remember—negative thoughts replaying in my head throughout my waking hours as well as in my dreams. If you've ever had a song stuck in your head, imagine having to contend with that—in the form of negative dialogue—twenty-four seven. I could be cooking or driving and suddenly cuss out loud, startling myself and others around me. Those of us who suffer with them understand how intense they can be. If you have ever encountered someone delusional who screams aloud because they hear imaginary voices in their head, you would probably avoid them like the plague. Well, the only difference between delusions and ruminations is that the latter is reliving experiences that are real. Sadly, my mother suffered from both delusions and ruminations. I can still picture her preparing dinner in our kitchen. She could be heard shouting at imaginary voices one minute, and shortly thereafter, she would be reenacting an argument she had with my father. My ruminations fall into three categories: past, present, and future:

Past

Ruminations stemming from my past involve images of people's faces (including my own reflection when I was anguished or physically injured), toxic dialogue, and other traumatic events going back to early childhood. I have often felt cursed with the ability to recall every hurtful word and phrase ever spoken to me, many in my native tongue. Most are filled or laced with profanity, but here are some examples with clean language:

Giving birth to you was my biggest mistake!

Go back to China! (heard recently, for the umpteenth time)

This is our secret.

This is what we do to animals (as I was being paddled by the head nun/principal).

You will just end up in jail or dead (quote from my middle school homeroom teacher).

Tell anyone and I'll kill you (as a bully is pressing a switchblade against my cheek).

Move an inch and I'll blow your brains out (as a shotgun was pointed near my head).

I used to envy characters on television and in movies who suffered from amnesia. Being able to wipe my memory clean, then starting over with a clean slate was something I constantly fantasized about.

Present

*I*ntrusive thoughts about the present involve presumptions that I am being criticized, judged, or disrespected, which are usually unfounded. Other annoyances occur when my OCD is in overdrive, which causes me to second-guess myself, worry obsessively, procrastinate, get stuck in rituals, strive for perfection, attempt to control everything, and beat myself up. I also become consumed with fear, and over-analyze things, replaying different scenarios in my head over and over again.

Future

*T*houghts and images of confrontations that I fear will occur, along with excessive worrying about the future, make up the final group. Past, present, and future ruminations are interrelated as my fears about what will befall me can be directly linked to past traumas. Constantly feeling vulnerable has caused me to be hyper-vigilant at all times, expecting violence or tragedy to occur at any moment. I have been praised for being able to react well in crisis situations, but this stems from never feeling safe. Having my guard up at all times eventually took its toll on both my physical and emotional well-being.

(My ruminations, like flashbacks, can also be triggered by conflicts and stress. I have often wondered if the constant racing thoughts in my head could be unconscious attempts to block ruminations and other negative thoughts from emerging.)

*F*ollowing my mindfulness insight regarding Johnny, I took the same path with ruminations as they occur by practicing compassion to cultivate forgiveness. I viewed each incident from the other party's perspective, accepted responsibility for my actions, and sought closure by *asking for* or *offering* forgiveness. If I harbored any anger or resentment toward those who harmed or offended me, it helped for me to visualize the other person(s) as a vulnerable child. If necessary, I focused on how we're interconnected. I would ask myself, *What if my son or a close friend said or did the same thing to me? Would I be more tolerant or accepting? Would I be as quick to regard the person as an enemy?* If responding to a particular intrusive thought with compassion and forgiveness was still a challenge for me, I summoned my Nurturing Parent to comfort and reassure my Adapted Child who was still suffering. I knew from experience that forcing the issue would be counterproductive. So I let it go and readdressed the rumination at a later time. By then, in most cases, my mindfulness practice provided additional clarity and insight, and my Adapted Child was at a better place to transform the anger.

    Ruminations often emerge during inopportune moments. If I'm having a conversation with someone and it triggers something negative from my past, I implement mindfulness immediately to intersect the thought. A little focus, a few deep breaths, and no one even notices.

*Y*ears ago, when I was working the 12 Steps as part of my addiction recovery, I made a list of people I had harmed and attempted to make amends to them or ask for their forgiveness, either directly or indirectly. My mindfulness practice helped me realize that my Step work fell short. For one thing, ruminations associated with people that I harmed persisted without any noticeable change. Also, many additional faces and images have surfaced. Most of them were people that I had harmed going back to kindergarten and had conveniently suppressed in my memory—some for nearly fifty years. As of this writing, I have addressed hundreds of these past acts. Initially, it was hard to fathom purposely evoking ruminations to emerge, but that was what I concentrated on during my hikes and other meditation sessions. And when they surfaced, I embraced them with gratitude.

Chapter 10

Healing My Adapted Child

I noticed the benefits from practicing compassion and forgiveness almost immediately, which served as a strong motivator to continue the path. Once I addressed a specific flashback or rumination, its rate of recurrence dropped significantly; many have not resurfaced at all. I also gained insight into the dynamics of forgiveness and boundaries. Forgiving individuals who hurt me in the past doesn't mean I want them (physically) in my life. In fact, it means I am no longer allowing the negativity associated with them to occupy my thoughts (more on this later).

There are obviously different approaches that one can take when it comes to forgiveness. Several therapists that I worked with in the past had urged me to forgive others in order to move on. In other words, I should do it for my benefit. This logic made practical sense to my Adult ego state and I ran with it. However, I discovered that I was merely attempting to forgive in order to forget, which only brought short-term relief from the trauma. Eventually, I concluded that both my Nurturing Parent and Adapted Child must be involved. The compassion for those who harmed me emanates from my Nurturing Parent, yet *true forgiveness must come from my Adapted Child*, who had been harboring the pain.

Practicing mindfulness alone can keep my PTSD symptoms at bay. They can be maintained at arm's length in my unconscious mind, but they could be triggered unwittingly at any given moment, which has often been the case. In the same vein, I don't agree with the notion that time heals psychological trauma. It is my belief that time merely pushes the trauma into the unconscious where it lies dormant. The likely scenario is that in time it will re-emerge. Pema Chödrön writes in her book, *When Things Fall Apart: Heart Advice for Difficult Times*, "Nothing ever goes away until it has taught us what we need to know." I seem to be the poster child for that credo. However, by practicing mindfulness and combining it with Buddhism, along with the application of psychotherapeutic techniques, I have been able to switch from a reactive response to being proactive. In doing so, I have tamed and even *released* many of my symptoms (details will follow in the next chapter on Tonglen). I am continuing in this path, embracing nightmares, flashbacks and ruminations as they surface. When I experience nightmares now, I am startled, initially, but have trained myself to implement my practice starting with mindfulness. I'm usually groggy and a bit traumatized, but taking deep breaths and focusing on the present moment fosters calmness. Next, I summon my Nurturing Parent for comfort and support. Depending on my frame of mind, my Nurturing Parent will either guide me to respond to the trauma associated with the nightmare, or comfort me back to sleep. I have discovered that if the nightmare isn't addressed right away, remnants of it typically reappear again within a day or two during my hike, where the trauma associated with the dream can be embraced.

Chapter 11

Tonglen: The Power of Compassion

*T*onglen, a Tibetan word that translates as "giving and taking," is a popular Buddhist meditation practice done to awaken one's own compassion by embracing the suffering of all living beings. The technique is commonly taught by visualizing the pain, illness, or struggles of oneself or others on the in-breath, and sending out relief/happiness on the out-breath. Practicing Tonglen is also a way to cultivate nonattachment, egolessness, and selflessness.

Practitioners are usually instructed to begin by addressing their own suffering. Once we're comfortable with this, we are encouraged to focus on someone else, such as a relative or close friend. Next, a distressed stranger would be chosen. Finally, Tonglen is practiced to benefit someone who is disliked or regarded as an enemy. Hence, doing Tonglen can be both rewarding and intense.

When I first devoted myself to Buddhism, Tonglen meditation was a huge challenge. First, I had been repeatedly taught that it was unhealthy to visualize breathing in negative energy during meditation. Second, I had a difficult time embracing suffering on behalf of someone I disliked. As far as I was concerned, it was no different than asking me to take a bullet for someone I despised. So my Tonglen meditation in the first year was haphazard. Eventually, the calmness I attained from mindful hiking, combined with the teachings of interbeing, along with the benefits I realized addressing flashbacks and ruminations—convinced me of the healing power of empathy and compassion. Henceforth, I opened myself to Tonglen.

Presently, I practice Tonglen on a daily basis as part of my evening sitting meditation regimen. I begin with mindful breathing for my own benefit. Next, I make a selection from what I call my Tonglen *circle*, a roster of people or groups chosen to be the beneficiaries of my prayers. Once I identify a recipient, I visualize the person encased by dark fumes and breathe them in. During the momentary pause before exhaling, which I call the *mid-breath*, I imagine billowing, white smoke dissipating the fumes (occasionally, I sprinkle healing dust in lieu of white smoke). As I'm breathing out, I picture my recipient emancipated and filled with joy.

My Tonglen circle was initially made up of family and close friends; neighbors and acquaintances were added next. In regard to strangers, I prayed for victims of recent natural disasters that I read about. When I was ready to add individuals I disliked or considered an enemy, the first person who came to mind was Johnny, my assailant from the past. I continued to view him as someone who, like me, endured abuse in the past and most likely still suffered.

Chapter 12

Releasing the Trauma

*E*arlier, I described how forgiving Johnny by transforming anger into compassion reduced my PTSD symptoms associated with him considerably. After I selected Johnny for Tonglen meditation, my nightmares and flashbacks of his assault stopped *altogether*. I have no idea if Johnny is still living, yet I have adopted him as one of my spiritual gurus. Now, when I become anxious about something or someone, I will practice Tonglen right away. This usually prevents negative experiences from reappearing as ruminations. When images of past altercations surface, I place those antagonists in my circle. My belief is that embracing so-called enemies in my Tonglen circle alters my Adapted Child's perception of them—from adversaries to being part of my spiritual community. This is what interconnectedness is all about and why I believe cultivation of compassion promotes the release and healing of past traumas once and for all. I call this "eternal forgiveness." Practicing Tonglen has awakened my heart and mind, bringing me closer to my inner Buddha. It has allowed me to declare a cease-fire in my private war against what I perceived to be a cruel world—beginning when I was a little boy.

When I took part in the gang war that culminated in the massacre in Chinatown, the brutal violence pushed my survival instincts into the darkest regions. Kidnappings, tortures, and killings became a way of life for me. Fighting, which had been my coping mechanism, was evolving into something akin to an addiction. Violence was how I self-medicated to deal with the trauma, which only led to more trauma and violence. It was maddening. I developed a dehumanized perception of my enemies, not unlike soldiers engaged in war. After I left the gang life, my fear and hatred of rival gang members did not diminish. In my mind, in order to survive (while unconsciously following my life script), they would remain my enemies for life. My magga empowered me to release that hatred.

Following my Tonglen breakthrough involving Johnny, I recognized the interconnectivity between myself and all the other rival gang members who were my sworn enemies. My adapted child recognized that I had more in common with them than most of my close "civilian" friends back then. We were angry young men coping with our emotional pain and insecurities by seeking empowerment in gangs. We wanted to make up our own rules and we wanted money to come fast and easy. We were rebelling against our parents as well as the elders who controlled the politics and money in the community. Our goals were identical: we were fighting each other to control the rackets in Chinatown. I can still picture many of my former enemies' faces, frozen in that time period. So I added them as a group to my Tonglen circle. I forgave them, asked for their forgiveness, then prayed for the relief of their suffering. After my first book, *Chinese Playground,* was published, two of my former gang associates, whom I hadn't seen in over twenty years, showed up with others at my book launch party. They made veiled threats against me for writing an exposé of the Chinese underworld—drawing unwanted attention to the gang—including members who were (and are) still imprisoned. Instead of remaining bitter, I have added these former comrades to my Tonglen circle as well.

I had been estranged from my mother since 1993. On the morning of June 24, 2009, I received a phone call from my son, informing me that she had passed away. I had just returned home from a cardio workout and my first reaction after hearing the news was that I needed to get on a hiking trail.

My earliest memory is of being consumed with fear that my parents would die. This thought quickly developed into an obsession and ranks, by far, as my longest-running rumination. It did not abate until my father died in 1992. I was thirty-eight at the time. Over the better part of the next twelve months, I made daily visits to his gravesite, often nibbling on lunch and chatting with his spirit. When I met my second wife in 1993, her views on pedophiles along with insight I gained from therapy empowered me to hold my father accountable for his past abuses. This was a difficult process, as it would have been easier to continue making excuses for him or to be in denial. In accordance with Chinese tradition, I was expected to honor my parents, without exception. This is a fundamental flaw in my culture, as it enables all forms of abusive behavior.

Although my perspective of my father changed following my awakening, I still worried about how I would deal with my mother's death, which was really about my fear of abandonment. I expected to break down and grieve during my hike, but I didn't shed a tear. What occurred was my first mindfulness insight. It became clear to me that I had already grieved the loss of my mother—many years ago. I know now that if I had bonded with my parents in a healthy way as an infant, I would not have been so terrified of losing them. These days, I devote a great deal of my Tonglen meditation to my parents, praying that they are each finally at peace.

*O*ne of the most agonizing memories I have doesn't involve violence or verbal conflict, yet it ranks up there in intensity; it is the dream and flashback that used to crop up most often. It was just a matter of time until the image appeared while I was hiking.

Picture a father and his young son walking through their quiet neighborhood in the early morning. The scene appears innocent enough; even endearing. However, it is approaching three a.m. on a weekday and, although he didn't do anything wrong, the second-grader is consumed with feelings of helplessness and guilt.

Desperate to spend time with him, I used to tag along with my father to nearby gambling parlors in Chinatown. Typically, I would watch the mahjong action for a few hours, and then drift off to sleep on one of the worn, lumpy sofas covered with cigarette burns. On the short walk home, I could tell by the way my father held my hand whether he came out ahead or was on the short end—losing money our family desperately needed to put food on the table. His grip wasn't particularly limp or firm—it just felt cold and distant. I sensed my father's anguish and felt helpless that I couldn't comfort him. I knew that it was best to keep my mouth shut and pretend I was invisible. Yet, I internalized his vibes, convincing myself that I was to blame. *I brought him bad luck with my presence. I jinxed him.*

Within a year, I would be pitching pennies and nickels against walls, and wagering my baseball cards in the schoolyard. Before long, gambling would become my "kryptonite," and remain so for the next forty-plus years. The recurring image and cold feeling of walking home, hand-in-hand, with my father would come up hundreds of times—like a self-torturous ritual—following many of my gambling binges.

As I became an adult in the eyes of the law and I began patronizing legal casinos, my response to the bonding image changed dramatically. Driving home alone, I cussed out loud at my father, blaming him for my vice. I accused him of passing the addiction to me, by exposing me to gambling. Years later, in recovery, I also held my father accountable for being a poor role model, by demonstrating that being *in action* was a convenient way to self-medicate.

For years, I have been sharing with my therapists and folks in recovery that I understood why my father gambled and that I didn't blame him for my addiction. I revealed the fact that my father was sold back in China when he was a little boy and this tormented him throughout his life. In TA terms, my Adult understood that my father's personal demons were perhaps more wicked than mine, while my Nurturing Parent had compassion for him. However, when I was on a gambling binge, I reverted to lashing out at my father, continuing to place all the blame on him. Although gambling had not been an issue for me for many years, this image still emerged when something triggered it, such as a news report on casinos or when I saw a man and a little boy walking hand-in-hand. Thanks to my magga, in particular Tonglen meditation (focused on my father), I have been able to release the suffering related to this memory.

(I also practice Tonglen for physical health. For instance, if I happen to be nursing a sore muscle, I will include Tonglen as part of my treatment. I begin by focusing on the injured area on the in-breath, visualizing dark matter surrounding the tissue. During the mid-breath, I imagine white smoke enveloping the darkened area. As I exhale, I picture the blended smoke exiting my body—repeating the exercise as appropriate.)

Chapter 13

Right Speech and Right Living

I recall passing the one-year mark of my magga and reflecting on how my life has evolved. I felt like I had been reborn, having adopted a lifestyle that enabled me to attain better control of my thoughts and emotions, gain both knowledge and insight, experience sensations of inner peace for the first time, empathize with others, and relieve much of my suffering.

An essential ingredient of this awakening is my practice of Buddhism, which entails abiding by the precepts to the best of my ability and committing to a path of wisdom, ethical conduct, and mental discipline. While mindfulness instills calmness and clarity, it is my devotion to studying and applying Buddhist teachings that cultivates kindness, compassion, openness, and insight. These are the key attributes that had been buried deep within me that I credit for the healing that has occurred so far.

Buddhist precepts are codes of conduct that are often compared to the Ten Commandments. Although there are numerous versions of precepts, they typically include the following: not killing any living beings, not stealing, not lying, refraining from sexual misconduct, abstaining from intoxicants, not praising oneself at the expense of others; and rightful speech. Buddhist precepts differ from commandments of the church in that violations of precepts do not result in punishment; nor are fear, shame, or guilt employed as deterrents.

Initially, the most challenging of the precepts for me was right speech, which is part of the Buddhist Eightfold Path to relieve suffering. The Buddha taught his followers that right speech has four parts: abstain from false speech; do not slander others; abstain from rude, abusive language; and do not indulge in gossip. I'm aware that for the majority of my life, I suffered from low self-esteem and lacked healthy coping skills. The worse I felt about myself, the more validation I sought. Unable to make much headway doing the inner work, I unconsciously focused on external ways to acknowledge myself that were mostly superficial and unkind. Judging and putting others down to elevate myself was part of my modus operandi. It is no wonder that abiding by right speech was such a challenge. However, tackling this issue forced me to take inventory of my attitude and behavior, and to realize that in order to practice kindness, I would first need to stop being *unkind*.

I made a conscious decision to halt my use of profanity, and to assess my speech before speaking—ensuring that what I had to say was true, kind, useful, and necessary. The result was that I found myself constantly catching myself before speaking since what was about to come out of my mouth was foul, cruel, condescending, or false. Before long, I thought my head was going to explode from the filtering and "verbal straightjacket" I strapped on myself. Fortunately, the discipline I developed from practicing mindfulness enabled me to stay focused and helped to release a lot of the tension. My early struggles to practice right speech led to an unexpected awakening. When I stopped resisting my verbal straightjacket, I came to appreciate those periods of silence. It was calming so I embraced them as additional opportunities to practice mindfulness as well as to reflect. This inspired me to take vows of silence on a regular basis as part of my magga.

When I reached the stage where I was consistently practicing right speech, I realized that abiding by this precept isn't just about diction. The practice is a way for me to end the war that I had launched against the world, including the maintenance of an extensive arsenal. Each time I judged, criticized, or verbally abused someone, I automatically *re-upped*, meaning I resupplied the toxic comments and negative energy in my armory with more of the same. This cycle reinforced my anger, fueled my war, and didn't leave any room for empathy or compassion. Negative speech draws negative energy, which pulls me further away from my inner Buddha and impedes my mindfulness practice.

I embrace right speech as another opportunity to cultivate compassion, which brings me closer to my true nature. Subsequently, I expanded the principles of right speech to my overall behavior (Right Living), ensuring that both my speech and actions are kind, useful, and necessary. By doing so, I am acting in accordance with the precepts and living a path of wisdom, ethical conduct, and mental discipline.

Chapter 14

Suffering and Addiction

Suffering is the core theme of Buddha's teachings known as the Four Noble Truths. While it seems logical that people do everything possible to avoid pain, discomfort, and distress, Buddhists have a totally different perspective: not to shun or fear it, but to regard it as part of life and an opportunity to awaken our compassion. Admittedly, there was a time when I mocked Buddhist monks as being masochists, never imagining that one day I would be touting their beliefs on this subject.

I have heard thousands of personal stories of suffering and closely observed how individuals dealt with it by self-medicating. Most of these disclosures came from fellow addicts who shared intimate details of their history of out-of-control gambling, alcohol, and drug use. A large number of us grew up in emotionally troubled homes where we were neglected or subjected to abuse in one form or another. Some learned to use intoxicants from their parents. Others disclosed that they had loving, supportive parents like June and Ward Cleaver, but a crisis or series of traumatic events—such as a sexual assault or military combat—crushed their spirits. Then there are those who deny they have a problem; these folks tend to bond with the "entitled" ones whom, by their own account, grew up rarely hearing the word, "No."

I have come to believe that addiction, in most cases, is the Adapted Child crying for help by acting out. Addicts, including me, who are at the mercy of our disease, are rebellious, illogical, cunning, manipulative, and resourceful. We will do anything to get our fix and any type of reasoning or rational input—including those from our Inner Adult—is resisted.

I have often shared in meetings that I was emotionally stuck in adolescence until I committed to my recovery. When I revealed this, there would usually be other members nodding their heads up and down. Family, friends, and colleagues of addicts view us as grown adults and expect us to act responsibly (understandably so), unaware that many of us function in the world as immature teens and not fully in control of our behavior. It isn't merely a coincidence that our tendency to make poor decisions and our inability to exercise restraint are issues that many adolescents face as well. Scientists believe the cause is attributed to immature prefrontal cortex.

I have found that the most effective way to interact with other addicts and guide them is to establish clear, firm boundaries in a compassionate manner. And yes, it often requires repeating the word, "No!" Addicts may resent structure and being told what to do, but it's what we need as our lives have become unmanageable.

A popular hypothesis about addicts is that we *use* because we're seeking reward reinforcement, i.e. the dopamine effect. It is my belief that although many addicts started using for the thrill, excitement, euphoria, etc., we don't continue to use to feel good, but in order *not to feel bad*—which is quite different. In other words, we desperately want to avoid suffering—whether it's the physical symptoms of withdrawal or to keep our inner demons at bay. My drug of choice, which I discovered at around age eight, was gambling. Over a forty-year period of compulsive wagering, I rarely had fun or felt pleasure in gambling. But what I can attest to is that when I was *in action*, I (addicted) didn't feel a thing. Beginning in grammar school, gambling provided me with a temporary reprieve from the anguish I felt, which stemmed from family drama, stress (both ongoing and post-traumatic), self-hate, disappointments, rejections, and failures. In adulthood, I reacted to difficulties associated with career, marriages, fatherhood, and trauma in the same manner. When I gambled, I wouldn't quit while I was ahead because, subconsciously, I knew the numbness would wear off and I'd have to face the realities of my life again. So I gambled until every last dollar I could get my hands on was gone. Thoughts and images of my past were huge triggers for me, so I gambled as an escape, which created more nightmares, flashbacks, and ruminations. This cycle of madness repeatedly drove me into major depression, followed by mania (medical term is "mixed features"), which eventually brought me to the edge of suicide.

Of course, compulsive gamblers, alcoholics, and drug addicts aren't the only ones who numb themselves to avoid suffering. There are people who turn to food, sex, work, video games, television, and the Internet to cope with stress and emotional pain; others feed their inflated ego, hoard, shop

(Oniomania), cut or starve themselves for the same reason. One can easily draw the conclusion that many of us substitute (or attempt to control) one type of pain or problem for another. Psychologists regard this as engaging in maladaptive coping mechanisms.

I learned a tough lesson shortly after I began attending GA meetings in 1987. Constant urges to gamble were consuming me and I relied on the guidance of old-timers in the program. I was constantly told to take it, "one day at a time," so that's how I painstakingly tackled my recovery as a newbie. It is common knowledge that the first ninety days in recovery is brutal for most addicts. We have abruptly given up our drug of choice, which we had regarded as our best friend, lover, security blanket, and crutch; it served as an anesthesia, but had been gradually destroying us like a malignant tumor. The likelihood of developing a cross addiction during this initial "detox" period is high.

The first time I reached my ninety day anniversary, I was contending with strong urges. I spent the evening at a meeting, returned home and immediately got on the phone reaching out to other GA members. I finally went to bed thinking, *Thank God I made it through another day...one day at a time.* A few hours later, I woke up drenched in sweat, shaking uncontrollably—suffering symptoms of withdrawal. Within an hour, I was standing in front of an ATM machine across the street from a local card room. Gambling, like other addictions, is a progressive disease. So when I relapsed, I made up for the lost time—physically, emotionally, and financially. Eventually, I returned to GA with my tail between my legs and shared during therapy that, "A day at a time doesn't work for me. I need to work my recovery *one second at a time*." Of course, I would come to appreciate this even more sixteen years later, once I had begun to explore mindfulness.

When my second book, *Born to Lose: Memoirs of a Compulsive Gambler*, was published by Hazelden in 2005, I credited much of my recovery at that juncture to Gamblers Anonymous. On June 24, 2013, I celebrated ten years of being clean and sober from gambling. I am still an advocate of GA and 12-Step fellowships. As I stated earlier, Buddhism and the 12-Step recovery program share many similarities. However, due to my history of trauma, PTSD, and manic depression, which account for most of the underlying causes of my addiction, I discovered that integrating mindfulness, Buddhist teachings, and psychotherapy into my treatment protocol has enhanced its efficacy. For example, in the recovery program, I was taught to identify and avoid triggers. Well, nightmares, flashbacks, and ruminations have always been huge triggers in my gambling, and avoiding them was unrealistic. Nowadays, I don't solicit them, but when they emerge, I address them with mindfulness, insight, and compassion. Also, suicidal ideation is common among both compulsive gamblers and manic depressives. (Bipolar sufferers are reported to have the highest rate of suicide among all mental illnesses; an estimated twenty percent of us take our own lives.) With the best of intentions, 12-Step old-timers and my past therapists encouraged me to develop positive coping strategies in order to avoid and counter suicidal thoughts. Their suggestions included exercising, listening to music, pursuing my hobbies, engaging in fun activities, and utilizing laughter as medicine. None of these helped; in fact, when I engage in cardio exercise, my body produces and releases high levels of epinephrine, an adrenal hormone that is associated with the fight or flight response in both humans and animals. In the past, when it elevated and reached a certain point, I became agitated and hostile (practicing mindfulness has resolved this). As I reflect on this now, these activities targeted my Inner Free Child, the part that is carefree, playful, spontaneous, and uninhibited. Yet, it was my Adapted Child who was suffering. Thoughts of suicide were overwhelming me, until I followed Pema Chodron's advice to embrace them, smell them, feel them, analyze them, make friends with them—then release them.

The Third Step in the fellowship advocates turning our will and lives over (surrendering) to a power greater than ourselves (higher power). When I embraced Buddhism, I shifted my spiritual practice, focusing on awakening my inner Buddha—relying on the power *within* to cultivate compassion for myself and others. This empowered me to treat and release my Adapted Child's suffering, including my gambling addiction. Fundamentally, this is what attracted me to

Buddhism. The Dharma directs us back to ourselves. The Buddha presented himself as a teacher and instructed his followers to think for themselves and not take his words at face value. He did not wish to be worshipped.

I still see value in the 12-Step concept of surrendering, especially for newcomers in the program. I spent decades resisting recovery because my nature was not to trust anything or anyone. My ego was one of my defenses against what I perceived to be an unsafe world. Sadly, this prevented me from accepting help or admitting that my addiction had defeated me. My last relapse finally broke down my defenses and I finally admitted that I couldn't do it on my own. So I do believe that surrendering to the program is what many addicts seeking help need to do in order to get in touch with their humility and open up their hearts and minds. *YOU ARE NOT ALONE!*

The questions that I get asked most often relating to my gambling is, "How much did you lose altogether?" and "What's the most you lost at one time?" My answers have probably disappointed some people, but the reality is that my biggest losses have nothing to do with money. Financially, I was able to get back up on my feet after each relapse, but the time lost cannot be replaced. Precious moments that were spent gambling and not with loved ones are gone forever. Plus, when I was gambling heavily, even the times spent with family were unfulfilling, as my mind tended to be preoccupied with gambling urges or worries about finances—oftentimes both. Each relapse took heavy tolls on my mental state as well, leaving my psyche more fragile than before. A common phrase heard in GA is that, "Gambling only leads to jail, insanity, or death." I can definitely attest to that.

Mindfulness is a potent coping mechanism for me—not only to treat my addiction and other mood disorders—but to maintain a sense of equanimity. It has an immediate and direct link to my Adapted Child. Practicing mindfulness frees me to reach a higher consciousness where I can embrace insights and interpret what my gambling urges—as well other symptoms, such as ruminations, flashbacks, and impulsivities—are communicating to me. From there, I can cultivate compassion to awaken my heart and treat the real causes of my suffering.

I think it's important to differentiate mindfulness from willpower. I associate the latter with resistance.

It involves fighting things that are undesirable, such as temptations, cravings, urges, impulses, and even physical pain—through sheer force of will. Mindfulness, on the other hand, entails focusing on the present in order to sidestep or release the attachments (temptation, cravings, impulses, etc.). Also, by being completely focused on the present moment, mindfulness prevents other thoughts and images from forming. I view willpower and mindfulness as different forms of mental discipline. When my mind is calm and clear, I also gain insight, which allows me to embrace the attachment, greet it, examine it, learn from it, and then release it. For example, I have employed mindfulness in response to cravings for sweets. When I'm focused, I usually gain insight into what's going on in my life that triggered the craving; most of the time, it's because I'm anxious about something or feeling discouraged. Possessing this insight allows me to address the root cause.

> MINDFULNESS MEANS SELF OBSERVATION. YOU CAN FEEL ANY FEELING WITHOUT HAVE TO ACT ON IT. WATCH THE FEELING AS AN OUTSIDE OBSERVER - NOTICE IT ONLY HAS POWER YOU CHOOSE TO GIVE IT!

Chapter 15

Attachments

*H*ow I chose to cope evolved throughout my lifetime and it involved attachments as well as cravings. When I was six, I had a small box that contained my prized possessions: one ping pong ball, a few marbles, a dented penny, an empty red (*lai see*) envelope saved from Chinese New Year, and about a dozen baseball cards. When my mother and father fought or other drama unfolded in our home, I would go and organize my box, attempting to maintain a sense of control in my life. During this period, I was constantly washing my hands until they bled. After I turned eight, I gambled away my baseball cards and the benign items in the box were replaced with ominous objects, such as knives, car hood ornaments (sharpened into weapons), skeleton keys, and stolen property—all of which represented the escalating turmoil and violence in my life. Shortly after being falsely accused of shoplifting, I actually began learning the art of "five-finger discounting" and fenced the stolen goods. I sought empowerment by joining street gangs. I peddled illegal fireworks, robbed customers, and stole from my own family—primarily to fund my gambling. If you're wondering if the false shoplifting charge was responsible for launching my criminal career, I can assure you that I was already on the path of delinquency.

After giving up the gang life and graduating from college, I went "legit." Licensed card rooms, Nevada casinos, and the stock market replaced the illegal gambling I had done in back alleys, pool halls, and other "dark" venues. Following my separation and divorce, I became a workaholic because gambling wasn't providing enough of an escape for me. After becoming involved in Gamblers Anonymous, I went through periods of abstinence, where I found myself accumulating "stuff," including prime real estate and a luxury car. We live in a culture where having a strong work ethic is considered a virtue, and accumulating material possessions represents success; but as the saying goes, "There are two sides to every coin." In my case, I had simply replaced one group of unhealthy attachments and cravings with another.

In 1999, while working the Steps in the recovery program, I was inspired to re-evaluate and transform my life. Hence, I made another futile attempt to practice Buddhism. Compulsive gamblers are advised in GA literature not to make any major life changes within the first two years of recovery. This made perfect sense to me. We need to focus on our recovery—in order to avoid the added stress that often accompanies life events, such as a job change, moving, making a major purchase, starting a romance, having a child, and so on. Since I had started my new "clean" date in 1997, over twenty-four months had passed and I was anxious to get a fresh start. I sold my home, gave away most of my possessions, and took a sabbatical from my consulting practice—where I had been averaging seventy-five to eighty-hour work weeks. But this ended horribly, due to the fact that I had removed my coping methods without truly addressing the underlying issues of my addiction and suffering.

As my spiritual path leads me closer to my inner Buddha, I have found it easier to let go of the things, both tangible and intangible, that I had relied on—to feel safe, to avoid suffering, and to validate myself.

When I release the attachments now, the difference is

that I do not become anxious or feel compelled to replace them.

When I become upset, the cause can usually be traced to either expectations or my ego—both are impalpable attachments. I have set ideas about how things should be done and how people should act. This is part of my survival instinct. By embracing interconnectivity, I am able to recognize the bond I share with others, which cultivates openness and acceptance in how unique we are. I have a long way to go before I would ever describe my disposition as flexible or easygoing. However, I'm more open-minded and getting better at not taking unmet expectations personally.

Reducing my fears has been liberating. No longer do I need a weapon to feel safe, and no longer do I worry that I am unable to control my emotions and behavior. My ego requires less stroking. I don't always have to be right or place the blame on others; I don't need to get the last word in, or act like a big shot. I have less need to be in control, to seek approval, to be perfect, to come in first, to impress others, or be the center of attention. I'm able to admit when I'm wrong and apologize when it's called for, without being concerned about appearing soft or weak.

Chapter 16

Toxic Karma: Treating Children as Commodities

I'm pretty sure he was tall and wore a dark suit. I definitely recall him being white, handing me a quarter, and saying, "Good job." That was the first money I ever earned and the first time anyone paid me a compliment. The fact that it was merely for polishing his shoes didn't matter to me. I was four and accompanying my older brother at a park bordering the financial district. "10¢" was scribbled on the side of our rudimentary wooden shoe shine box. I was being taught to read people, differentiating prospective customers from other folks: window shoppers, snitches, and those with ulterior motives, specifically—pedophiles. I was also learning a vital lesson: how to increase both the probability and size of gratuities by smiling and acting cute. More importantly, I remember this as the first time I exploited myself as an object.

In consideration of the fact that my parents attempted to abort me, you can say that the "commodity seed" was planted in me before my birth. I often wondered how my mother felt after the botched abortion. Was she disappointed in what is now referenced in medical terms as a "continuing pregnancy?" Did she experience an epiphany and embrace me as a fetus growing inside of her? This was one of many topics that were off limits in my family so I never brought it up. When I attended the self-parenting workshop after college, one of my fellow attendees provided me with some insight on this. We were covering the topic of prenatal communication—the bonding between mothers and fetuses. Another attendee, I'll call him "Colin," estimated to be in his late '20s or early '30s, shared a powerful story with the group. To summarize, he stated that, although his mother was consistently affectionate and loving toward him, deep down he always felt unwanted. Colin said that as far back as he could remember he has been haunted by a recurring dream. In it, Colin hears his mother, pregnant with him, praying to God—expressing her indecision about whether she should keep the baby or put it up for adoption. Colin told us that he recently revealed the dream to his mother, including the exact words she spoke. Colin said his mother immediately broke down in tears and confirmed that when she was pregnant, she drove to a field where she stood alone and prayed aloud to God. The dialogue in his dream was near verbatim to what she said, which has haunted her as well. My fellow attendee finished his story by disclosing that the confirmation from his mother was the motivation for him to enroll in the workshop.

I don't recollect any telepathic communication between my mother and me before I was born, but Colin's story dimmed lingering hopes I had that my mother embraced the pregnancy at any time. And nearly being sold after I was born reinforced the notion that it was probably easier for my parents to perceive me as an object—and not a person.

When I was nine, I grudgingly stood in small claims court next to my father, in a case against one of our tenants. The judge began the proceedings by inquiring why I wasn't in school, and I replied that I was there to serve as my father's interpreter—reassuring him that I planned to head straight to class from the courthouse. But that was only part of the reason for my presence there. You see, although I was the baby of the family, I had been designated as the property manager. Each time I protested, my father made it clear that I did not have a choice—it was my obligation. I know my father loved me, but his belief that his children existed to serve him—in every way he desired—was even stronger. His expectations were gradually incorporated into my life script, which I played out as an honorable son, even after he died. I'm a firm believer in family members all pitching in, developing good work ethics and character, but what was demanded of me had nothing to do with any of that.

Another family secret is that my father sexually abused his children, including me. Once, when I was about thirteen, my father entered my room in the middle of the night while I was asleep. I awoke feeling my blanket being lifted and immediately started flailing my arms. My father proceeded to reassure me that it was him and that it was okay. Nevertheless, I kept swinging away even after I recognized who was there. Perhaps my father was merely covering me with the blanket as a loving gesture, but I couldn't be certain.

There were plenty of times when my father seemed genuinely concerned about my well-being, but it was unsettling because I knew that his inner demons could emerge in a flash if he felt slighted in the least bit. Once his demons took hold, I would immediately become his mortal enemy. I never felt totally safe in my father's presence. I often tried to imagine the abuses he suffered as a child that created his dark side.

I had very little sense of my true nature prior to committing to my spiritual practice. There were occasions throughout my lifetime when I surprised myself by instinctively doing what was moral, ethical, and selfless—but most of the time I was functioning from a dark place. I began the first chapter of this book by stating that for the majority of my life, my lifestyle was the antithesis of how Buddhists live. I was obsessed with winning, seeking approval, gaining popularity, advancing my career, accumulating wealth and possessions, and satisfying my cravings. By pursuing these superficial endeavors, I continued to treat myself as a commodity—alienating myself from my true nature—which is pure, compassionate, calm, peaceful, loving, and charitable. Growing up, I had little interest or use for these attributes, as my focus tended to be on surviving my environment and the difficult choices I made. However, as time passed, my suffering continued to mount and the coping methods I relied on only created more problems.

I'm inspired when I see parents nurture and encourage their children to explore their talents, develop positive attributes, and reach their potential, when this is carried out with the kids' best interest at heart. But I'm saddened when I see mothers and fathers pushing their children into activities and endeavors to satisfy the parents' own agenda. I have often wondered how child actors, sports phenoms, and other young entertainers stay grounded and discover their inner qualities and true nature, when the public—and even their handlers—treat them as objects. Conversely, there are individuals who treat (and pamper) inanimate objects such as cars better than people, leaving loved ones feeling inadequate.

Chapter 17

Keeping Things in Perspective: Road Rage and Bird Poop

I used to go psycho when another motorist: tailgated me, cut me off, high-beamed me, honked their horn, gave me the finger or flashed me a perceived dirty look. I have chased cars down on the freeway and duked it out with a stranger on the side of the road—someone who was apparently just as disturbed me. It's a wonder I didn't get myself killed or thrown in jail. After these altercations, I had mixed emotions. Part of me actually felt relieved having unloaded the pent-up anger, but I also hated myself and was terrified regarding my lack of self-control. The people I tangled with may have been frustrated with their boss or with a family member, the traffic, the lack of control in their lives, or they might have been grieving over the loss of something or someone. My issues, however, ran deeper than that. When I got behind the wheel, my ego became inflated and I expected other drivers to behave in a manner that suited *me*. My aggressive behavior attracted and triggered the kindred energy of others. I thought I was in control, but operating a vehicle exposed my vulnerability. I was a ticking time bomb on four wheels. I perceived these insolent drivers as the people in my past who bullied me or treated me like I was a burden.

My son kept me out of a lot of trouble. His mother and I shared custody of him from the time he was eighteen months old and his presence had a calming effect on me. Not wanting my child to turn out like me was a great motivator for me to be on my best behavior around him.

Since becoming a lay Buddhist and making a commitment to address my suffering, I no longer view the road as a battleground. On this path, I have discovered ways to be a courteous, compassionate driver. The first thing I do when I get in my car is mindful breathing. As I turn the ignition and start the car, I am usually greeted by the voice of Pema Chödrön. I like to have one of her audio recordings loaded in the sound system. Her teachings are profound, yet it is her soothing voice and serene disposition that has a calming effect on me. It's like having a Nurturing Parent in the car with me. Alternatively, I listen to classical music. It's not my favorite genre, but the tranquil sound is beneficial for my temperament.

I used to practice mindful breathing during traffic stops. Now it's something I do throughout the day—even when I'm driving—which keeps me calm and alert on the road. My definition of time management has changed as well. These days, it doesn't involve multi-tasking or competing to get more done in an hour or day than anyone else. Instead, it means that I focus on one single task and give myself extra time to complete it in order to practice patience. Being courteous to other motorists is part of my spiritual practice, which allows me to fulfill my daily quota of performing acts of kindness.

It's amazing how four fingers can mean the difference between peace and war. When I accidentally cut someone off on the highway, or need to switch lanes in a hurry, I always raise my hand and wave—

signaling my apology or to express my gratitude. This gesture may seem trivial, but waving represents acknowledgment of my error, respect for the other driver, and a non-threatening presence. It worked on me when I was on the other end and about to go berserk. At times, other drivers will sound their horn a split second before I raise my hand up or they will press their horn anyway. In the past, I would instinctively react by flipping them off; now, I wave my hand and repeat if necessary.

Another driving etiquette I practice is not to look over at another driver unless I intend to smile at them. If I become irritated or upset at another driver, I practice mindful breathing and keep my eyes on the road. In the past, I wouldn't hesitate to give the evil eye, which has led to confrontations. What also helped me to release my road rage was a conscious decision to use my car horn strictly for safety reasons. The old Bill used to pound on the horn as soon as the traffic signal turned green. My thinking these days is that if the driver ahead of me doesn't proceed immediately and the delay means I will sit through another traffic signal cycle, I embrace the time as an opportunity to practice mindfulness. No big deal.

I used to regard the above techniques as being submissive or passive—when in fact they're empowering. I realize now that for most of my life, when I became anxious or upset, I was relinquishing my power. Many years ago, I was taking a walk and a small glob of bird poop landed on my head. You may have experienced this, but my guess is that your reaction was quite different from mine. Well, I became enraged and searched long and hard for that bird. I wanted to find and kill it. I even planned to return the following day at the exact same time armed with a BB gun. I was reminded of this incident recently, because it happened again; only this time, I embraced the memento on my head as a cue to focus on mindful breathing. I took it as a reminder for me to practice humility as well. I reflected on the earlier experience and recognized the absurdity of allowing a tiny bird so much power over me. This same logic applies to my past meltdowns on the road as well and for most of the altercations throughout my lifetime. I began this book recounting the incident with the blind fellow at the all-hands meeting. I got myself all worked up and the other person didn't even know I was alive. You can imagine the times I forfeited my power to someone (or something) who didn't even ask for or want it. I am beginning to appreciate the potency of turning the other cheek and walking away as a way to cultivate kindness and compassion for others as well as for myself. This is definitely a path I prefer over cultivating anger and violence.

Chapter 18

Mindful Consumption and Maintenance

Mindful Consumption is another term coined by Thich Nhat Hanh. It underscores the importance of being cognizant of what we allow in both our bodies and minds. I take this concept to heart, and pay close attention to what I eat, hear, see, touch, smell, and taste—ensuring that they are all in accordance with Buddhist precepts and my spiritual practice. The manner in which I choose to live determines the progress and efficacy of my magga. This includes being fully astute regarding my cravings and attachments. Following are some of the ways that I practice mindful consumption:

Intoxicants

I abstain from taking intoxicants and I avoid social gatherings where they will be consumed. This may seem extreme, yet it is a lifestyle choice that works for me, since I correlate intoxicants with "unmindfulness."

Media

I no longer watch my favorite television programs or genre of film, simply because they're not conducive to the path I'm on. In one form or another, movies and shows such as *The Godfather, GoodFellas, The Sopranos, and Sons of Anarchy* reinforce how I used to either think or live. Although I was aware that viewing them triggered some of my symptoms, I continued to indulge in them because, unconsciously, they allowed me to reminisce about the past, providing my fragile ego with a quick and easy boost. Following my commitment to Buddhism, I realized that these programs pushed me further away from my true nature. So now I refrain from watching overtly violent shows and those that glamorize criminal, immoral, or unethical behavior.

In high school, I used to sneak off on my own to watch foreign films by directors such as Lina Wertmuller, Claude Berri and François Truffaut. Their movies were character-driven and thought-provoking, remaining with me long after the credits rolled. It appears that I've come full circle in my quest to find worthwhile entertainment as my Netflix queue is comprised mostly of titles from foreign and independent studios.

I grew up listening to Motown ballads in the '60s and '70s, and my musical taste remained the same into the new millennium. In addition to enjoying the slow melodies, the lyrics allowed me to wallow in my grief when I was contending with loneliness, heartbreak, anxiety, confusion, loss, or despair. At times, I felt as though these emotions were conspiring and ganging up on me all at once. Of course, one can get too entrenched in melancholy. Plus, the tunes often conjured up vivid images of my toxic and violent past. I used to blast my speakers, unconsciously attempting to drown out my thoughts, whereas now I relish soft, tranquil music.

Television news reports often contain over-the-top graphics, specifically when it comes to reporting crimes. What works for me is to keep up with current events via online new sites, where I can scan and select articles of interest, usually foregoing the accompanying videos.

Competition

My participation in competitive sports began as a member of the twelve and under softball and basketball teams at the local playground. I soon discovered that it wasn't really about building character, learning good teamwork, sportsmanship, and improving physical fitness. No, it was all about the "W" and "L". And in my mind, winning meant I wasn't lame, and losing confirmed that I was worthless. This was the genesis of my "winning at all costs" approach to sports, fighting, crime, work, and life in general.

I played competitive tennis for twenty-five years. Actually, "acting out" on the tennis court would be a more accurate description of my participation. One day, while I was relaxing at a tournament, a young woman sitting next to me turned and said, "Would you mind if I ask you a question?"

"Sure," I replied.

"Do you guys play for money?"

"No, there isn't any prize money in these types of tournaments," I said. "In fact, we pay an entry fee."

"Well then, I'm confused. I recently started dating that guy playing over there. We had to get up really early this morning and drove over an hour to get here by eight a.m. Since I've been here, all I see and hear are guys yelling at themselves and arguing with their opponents. Not a single person seems to be enjoying themselves. Why do you do it?"

I opened my mouth to respond, but I was speechless. And she wasn't done.

"All I have to say is, he's acting like a jerk out there and I don't want to have anything to do with him."

I would have liked to point out to her that the players' behavior she witnessed was an aberration, but the truth is that competitive sports often reveal character defects. This applies to both players and spectators. When I competed in sports and everything else in life, unconsciously I perceived myself more as a machine than a person. My body and mind were used in competition to measure and validate myself.

It took many years for me to admit that competition—be it sports or a game of Scrabble—brought out the worst in me. I only acknowledged this when I was good and ready to change. As a sports-viewing fanatic for most of my life, the action was another convenient way to temporarily hide from myself with external stimulation. Nowadays, I rarely follow sports and prefer to partake in games without keeping score.

Diet, Exercise and Natural Mood Stabilizers

I regard maintaining a healthy diet and sticking with my exercise regimen as though each was essential medication, so I do not allow myself to skip or cheat on them. One of my birth defects is mitral valve prolapse, a disease of the heart, which results in regurgitation (backflow of blood). A loud murmur and enlargement of the left ventricle was discovered at age four when my appendix burst. I underwent an angiogram in 1964 when I was ten, which was inconclusive. In the mid-90s an echocardiogram identified the MVP with severe regurgitation. The defect has actually been a blessing. In spite of the initial prognosis of eventual open-heart surgery to repair or replace the valve, I decided that I had had enough of hospitals and scalpels—committing to stay fit in order to strengthen my heart muscle and myocardial function. A desire to keep a step ahead of surgery has been a strong motivator for me. I have applied this same fitness discipline to my spiritual practice.

It took me over a year to wean off Seroquel (Quetiapine Fumarate), an atypical antipsychotic medication approved as a mood stabilizer for the treatment of bipolar disorder. It had been prescribed to me for nearly ten years. After being completely off of Seroquel, it took another fourteen months to re-establish a normal sleep pattern. With the exception of being prescribed a low dosage (5 mg.) of fluoxetine (Prozac) daily as a migraine prophylaxis, I have been weaned off all psychotherapeutic medications. My psychiatrist continues to be supportive of my personal natural "cocktail" to treat my mood disorders. It consists of my spiritual practice, therapy, getting adequate sleep, exercise, sunshine, and Omega 3 from both fish oil and (ground) flaxseed. I find that it is better for me, both mentally and physically, to be in sync with my body's internal clock. I do this by maintaining a consistent schedule throughout the week for waking up, eating meals, snacking, exercising, meditating, and going to bed.

Conclusion

When my pdoc (slang for psychiatrist), Dr. L., who also serves as my therapist, informed me during one of our sessions that my bipolar disorder was in remission, I should have been pleased but, instead, I thought it was ironic. That's because I was just about to broach the subject of increasing my medication or perhaps switching to another mood stabilizer. I had been weaning off of Seroquel and was just one "step-down" away from being off of it completely. I may have met the psychiatric diagnostic criteria for remission, but I had been experiencing higher levels of anxiety in recent times and was concerned about my impulsivity. Dr. L., who bears a resemblance to music producer David Foster, listened to my concerns and his advice to me was to maintain my current dosage of Seroquel and to increase it on an as-needed basis. Shortly after this session, I began my spiritual practice. The timing was fortuitous, or perhaps I knew something had to be done about my issues, and I questioned whether increasing my medication was the best course of action. My decision to explore hiking occurred at an auspicious time.

I did not share my commitment to Buddhism with my pdoc right away. I wasn't sure if I could stick with it or what, if any, benefits would result. But once I informed him, Dr. L. was very supportive and wanted to know details about my magga. In subsequent sessions, he monitored my progress attentively, expanding his note-taking considerably following my revelation. Dr. L. logged his observations directly onto a desktop computer. At one point, when I was describing Tonglen meditation, I paused momentarily, wondering if he needed me to spell out the Tibetan word for him, but Dr. L. just kept pounding way at the keyboard. His head and eyes swung from side to side, making eye contact with me one moment, shifting over to his monitor the next, as if he was watching a tennis match. The doc perked up when I shared my perspective on the interconnection between Johnny and me, along with the techniques I used to pray for my former arch-enemy. Dr. L nodded his head when I reported that the recurring nightmares, flashbacks, and ruminations of Johnny had ceased. (As of this writing, they have not returned. Johnny remains in my

Tonglen circle and I pray for him on a regular basis. The image of him that emerges now is that of a little boy who is hurting both physically and emotionally.)

The integration of Buddhism and psychotherapy continues to gain popularity. There are psychotherapists who are ordained Buddhists, as well as therapists whose treatment modalities include mindfulness and other Buddhist concepts. I think it is important to stress to others being treated for a mood disorder or other mental illnesses that—any plans to adjust or augment your treatment plan should be discussed with your psychiatrist or therapist first—and to keep them apprised of any changes or concerns. A list at the end of this book includes a link where readers can search online for therapists by location, religious orientation, diagnosis, gender, treatment orientation, etc. In relation to finding a Buddhist teacher, I discovered that meditation centers and organizations that sponsor retreats are a good source for referrals. I have also included links to articles that may be useful.

Every now and again, someone will ask me, "Are you happy?" My reply is usually, "I'm doing okay" or "I'm doing better." When there is an opportunity to elaborate, I explain that happiness is not what I strive for. My focus, from moment to moment is to remain calm and stable. Unlike traditional Buddhists, I have no illusions about attaining enlightenment. That is not my goal nor has it ever been. My understanding of enlightenment is to be fully awakened and free of all attachments, including ego. Attaining this would mean the end of suffering, karma, and rebirth. I haven't embraced the concepts of past lives and rebirth as of yet, and I don't believe the end of suffering is realistic for me in this lifetime. However, I do fantasize about being free of *my* ego.

As I compose this last paragraph, I turn and glance at my date planner, which includes a notation for my next appointment with Dr. L. "FINAL!" is highlighted in red. I shake my head and grin as I reminisce about our first session, and how I nearly turned around and walked out of his office after less than ten seconds. I was suicidal at the time and part of me just wanted to end the suffering once and for all. I had been consumed with thoughts of leaping off the Golden Gate Bridge and that's where I wanted to be at that moment, instead of meeting a new pdoc. I was looking for an excuse to say, "Screw this," and take off. So when Dr. L. greeted me and introduced himself, I thought to myself, *I don't appreciate his tone of voice.* Little did I know that standing before me was the most qualified psychiatrist and therapist I would ever encounter. That fleeting moment when I wanted to abruptly walk out of his office would be the first and only time that I'd ever feel that way. That doesn't mean I've always felt warm and fuzzy in his presence. We've tackled some sensitive issues, as you can imagine. Having functioned as my therapist for nearly ten years, Dr. L. is now confident in my ability to navigate the ebb and flow of life. I am extremely grateful—both to him and for my magga.

Sources, Recommended Readings, and Other Information:

Books

When Things Fall Apart by Pema Chödrön

The Wisdom of No Escape by Pema Chödrön

Start Where You Are by Pema Chödrön

Finding The Still Point: A Beginner's Guide to Zen Meditation by John Daido Loori

Walking Meditation by Thich Nhat Hanh

The Art of Power by Thich Nhat Hanh

no death, no fear by Thich Nhat Hanh

Anger: Wisdom for Cooking the Flames by Thich Nhat Hanh

Taming the Tiger Within by Thich Nhat Hanh

Fear: Essential Wisdom for Getting Through the Storm by Thich Nhat Hanh

Games People Play by Eric Berne

Games Alcoholics Play by Claude Steiner

Pema Chödrön Audiobooks

Pure Meditation

Good Medicine: How to Turn Pain into Compassion with Tonglen Meditation

From Fear to Fearlessness

Internet Links

www.hazelden.org/itemquest/search.view?srch=Y&start=0&HAZLWEB_STORE_SELECTED=NONE&kw=born+to+lose

http://therapists.psychologytoday.com/rms/prof_search.php

http://www.naturalawareness.net/guidance.htm

http://buddhism.about.com/od/becomingabuddhist/a/retreats.htm

Gratitude

I would like to express my gratitude to Pema Chödrön and Thich Nhat Hanh. Their respective teachings and interpretation of the Dharma inspired me to begin my spiritual practice. To Dr. Lawrence Lanes: Your unwavering support and guidance have been a godsend. I am grateful to psychotherapist Isabel Mize and also to Marla Bergman, for their respective friendship, as well as for their time and efforts in editing the early drafts of the manuscript; and to Bianca Wulff for her kindness and help with polishing the manuscript. Special thanks to literary agent Susan Rabiner for continuing to share her expertise with me on publishing and for her input on the book title. I'd also like to extend my gratitude to all my friends and kind neighbors on "the hill."

About the Author

Bill Lee is a second-generation Chinese American who grew up in the underworld of San Francisco Chinatown. He is the author of *Chinese Playground* and *Born to Lose.* He has written for the S.F. Chronicle, AsianWeek, and numerous professional journals. Bill graduated with honors in Psychology from San Francisco State University and spent most of his career as a consultant retained by top executives in Silicon Valley. He has been featured on The History Channel, Fox, A&E Network, Spike TV, PBS, and Radio Television Hong Kong. You can visit his web sites at:

http://chineseplayground.com

http://facebook.com/Bill.Lee.author

Copyrighted Material

Excerpt from *Chinese Playground: A Memoir*

©1999-2014 by Bill Lee

Contents

Preface

Part One:

Chapter 1: Chinatown's Dirty Secrets

Chapter 2: Chinese Playground

Chapter 3: Keeping Up with the Wongs

Chapter 4: Hock Sair Woey, the Chinese Underworld

Chapter 5: Doin' the Nine-Ball Hustle

Chapter 6: "Riding the Water," Secret Society Executions

Chapter 7: Joe Boys

Chapter 8: The Golden Dragon Massacre

Part Two:

Chapter 9: A Chinese Soap Opera

Chapter 10: The Tao of Corporate Warfare

Chapter 11: High-Tech Warrior

Chapter 12: Massacre in Silicon Valley

Epilogue

Acknowledgments

About the Author

Preface

Chinese Playground began as an assignment for my psychology class in 1975. Undergraduate students were required to write an autobiography. Before submitting my work, I secured absolute confidentiality from my professor. Needless to say, he was shocked at the contents, which included an exposé on my family as well as the Chinese underworld.

After the Golden Dragon Massacre in 1977, followed by the subsequent arrests and convictions of my close friends, I was compelled to write my version of the Chinatown gang war under a pseudonym. I soon realized that my identity would be apparent and the risks were too great.

The fact remains that to my knowledge, there has never been a complete literary work presented from inside the Chinese underworld. Journalists, educators and sociologists have reported on specific crimes, conducted interviews or indirectly recounted experiences from former gang members. Facts were either inaccurate or voices of the characters diminished.

Following the ESL Massacre, I had a riveting story to share regarding the rampage and five-plus hours' siege. In compliance with a gag order issued on the case by the presiding judge, I decided to wait until Richard Farley's trial had ended before going public. After Farley was sentenced, I lacked the motivation and discipline to complete the project.

Writing this memoir during my emotional recovery allowed me to express myself honestly and with humility. The process served as a catharsis and was a milestone in my healing. Earlier versions would have been shallow, dark and arrogant.

Although a number of publishers (local and New York-based) expressed interest in the book, I decided to self-publish in order to retain my voice in the narrative. I discovered the literary world to be extremely subjective and the developmental input I received from agents and editors were inconsistent.

This is a true story about destiny, involving my dark journey through life. It is presented simply and straightforwardly. All events in the book occurred. Some names, dates and locations have been altered to protect the identities of victims and those who wish to remain anonymous.

Chapter 1. Chinatown's Dirty Secrets

Children love their parents unconditionally and naturally seek their approval. In the Chinese culture, we're taught as children to honor and obey our parents—no matter what. I never doubted my mother and father's love for my siblings and me. But in our home, the most horrible acts conceivable against children were also committed.

We never knew the exact age of my father. He was born in Toishan (Southern China) around 1908 into the Yee family. Due to severe financial hardships in his family, my father was sold as a young boy to Mr. Chin Wai and raised as his "No. 1 Son," Chin Bork Ngai.

The brokering of sons was common in Toishan, where many families were impoverished. Children, especially "sons," were regarded as valuable commodities. Couples with financial resources who were not able to bear male infants resorted to this practice in order to carry on the family legacy. Daughters were also sold. The lucky ones became servants, while others were sexually exploited.

My mother once shared with me that Grandpa Yee was a heavy gambler, which was the source of the family's problems. My father never talked about his birth parents, and we were supposed to pretend that the Yee family never existed. My mother said that although *Ah Yeh* (Grandpa Chin) provided a comfortable, loving home, my father never forgave his biological parents for giving him up.

The only time my father cried was in his sleep, when he would scream like a little boy in anger at Grandpa Yee for not wanting him. Once, when I was about ten, I ran to him and held him as he sobbed in his sleep. As my father awoke, he pushed me away and pretended everything was fine.

He loved Ah Yeh and his eyes gleamed when he spoke of *Ngen Ngen* (Grandma Chin), who spoiled and showered him with affection. Two other boys were born into the Chin household, which also included servants.

My father was well-educated and studied medicine in Guangzhou, the capital of Guangdong (Canton) province. Two large picture frames hung in our living room containing degrees and certificates he received in China. In 1949, Ah Yeh, like many other wealthy landowners, had his land and assets seized by the Communists. My father was sent to Hong Kong, an embittered man, who later devoted a good part of his life serving the Kuomintang Nationalist Party. There just had to be a way for him to get back at the Communists, who destroyed his home and family.

My mother's childhood is a puzzle and contains many secrets. Born and raised in Guangzhou, Chu Lau Han was the eldest of three. Her father was an acclaimed educator who built and directed a university in Guangzhou.

My mother idolized *Ghown Ghown* (Grandpa Chu)

as her hero, yet not a word was ever spoken about *Paw Paw* (Grandma Chu). When I inquired about her, my mother never responded.

At times, when my father became drunk and argued with my mother, he'd say, *"You're turning into your mother."*

She would either become silent and take it as a low blow, or snap back with something implying, *"You will never be the man my father was."*

No matter how angry any of the kids became, we knew better than to bring up the subject of Paw Paw to hurt my mother. That would have been a death wish.

My mother was fluent in at least three dialects of Chinese, including Mandarin. She was tutored by Ghown Ghown, completing her studies at his university. She was cared for by a nanny and, like my father, had the luxury of servants.

When the Japanese invaded Guangzhou during the Sino-Japanese War, Ghown Ghown remained at his university while Paw Paw escaped with the children.

Grandma Chin died unexpectedly, and my mother, who was nine at the time, became the caretaker for her baby brother and sister. They marched over a hundred miles to safety. The period from that time until she met my father, remains a mystery.

A number of possibilities have crossed my mind. *Perhaps Paw Paw was raped and murdered by soldiers. Could my mother have been abused in some way by soldiers or an acquaintance?* One thing was clear, she didn't trust anyone—not my father, her children, or even herself.

* * * *

The marriage of my parents was arranged. My mother had settled in Hong Kong with her siblings, eventually reuniting with Ghown Ghown, who was indigent after the war. My father, twice married before meeting my mother, had five children. His first wife died after a short illness and he remarried almost immediately. When he arrived home unexpectedly one day, he walked in on wife "No. 2" brutally beating the children and banished her.

My father first entered the United States in 1939 as a "paper son." Ah Yeh found a way around the Chinese Exclusion Act by arranging for a merchant with a surname of Lee to sponsor my father as his son. My father returned to China in '49 to take another bride, as the Communists were overrunning the country. With his five children scattered and cared for by various relatives, my father was seeking a better life in *Gum Shan,* or Gold Mountain (as California with its gold prospects was named by the Chinese).

Chu Lau Han, a beautiful woman with baby cheeks, fair skin and a mischievous smile, was eighteen when a matchmaker approached Ghown Ghown to discuss the prospects of a marriage and an opportunity to live in Gum Shan. The expectation, of course, was for the eldest to pave the way for the remaining Chu clan to join her in America.

As Ghown Ghown weighed the factors, the couple's

age difference of more than twenty years was an issue. My father's two prior marriages and five children were also considerations. The Communists' takeover had left him financially ruined. But in the end, Grandpa Chu could not pass up the opportunity for his Lau Han to emigrate to the U.S., so he gave his blessing.

My mother never had a boyfriend and knew nothing about men. She presumed Bork Ngai would love and adore her just like her father had. My mother was smitten with my father's handsome looks, self-confidence, and charming wit.

After one meeting, my mother and father were married in Hong Kong. It was early 1949. Their simple wedding included the traditional tea ceremony whereby my mother knelt in front of Ngen Ngen (her future mother-in-law) with her head bowed down, graciously offering a cup of tea. This ritual is a subtle way of saying, *Please accept me into your family.* It establishes the superior role of the mother-in-law from the outset. I wonder what Ngen Ngen's thoughts were, as this was the third ceremony she had endured for her eldest son.

My mother was in turmoil. She did not want to leave Ghown Ghown again. Yet she never questioned his decisions. She had a responsibility to the family, and what she wanted wasn't important. But leaving her home again to travel thousands of miles with a stranger she just married meant facing life's challenges unprepared. She didn't even know how to cook.

My mother had no idea how difficult life would be for her. Although my father would become one of the most powerful and respected men in San Francisco's Chinatown, he was also an alcoholic, compulsive gambler, womanizer, and much worse.

The remaining Chu clan never set foot in America. Lau Han never saw her loving father again. Her siblings slowly became strangers.

Bork Ngai and Lau Han arrived in San Francisco by boat in 1949. The journey took twenty-three days. By 1954, my mother had borne three girls and a boy. Mary was the first-born, followed by James, Dorothy and May. I was not yet in the picture.

My father worked out of the living room as a Chinese doctor and herbalist. Wood shelves against the kitchen wall were stacked with glass jars containing herbs in various forms: pill, bark, leaves, and powder. My mother, like many other immigrant women from China, worked as a seamstress. As frugal as they were, they were not able to make ends meet. Ah Yeh, who worked at a pawnshop where he also lived, helped as much as he could. Money had to be borrowed from friends.

* * * *

When my mother unexpectedly became pregnant with me, my father decided to abort me. Applying his medicinal training, he concocted a mixture of herbs, which he coerced my mother to ingest. His scheme failed. I was born on October 8, 1954, with serious birth and developmental defects. How they discharged me from the hospital as a healthy baby boy is a mystery.

Due to continuing poverty, my parents entered negotiations to sell me to a wealthy, childless couple. (This transaction would have been disguised as a private adoption. The brokering of children in China found its way to America.) However, a decision to keep me was apparently influenced by the emotional trauma my father endured as a child who was sold. The reality is that I would have been better off with another family.

Being left-handed was considered bad luck in our culture, so I was forced to eat and write with my right hand. Sharp taps to the knuckles served as reminders. My parents' resentment toward me was absorbed like a sponge.

Seven of us occupied a two-room apartment on the corner of Washington and Stockton streets, above Fun Loy Restaurant in the heart of Chinatown. We didn't have a refrigerator, had to heat our water on the stove and we shared beds. It was a typical ghetto tenement. Peeling paint dangled from the ceilings, hallways were morose and smelled of urine, and roaches outnumbered us at least a thousand-to-one.

There were twelve apartments in the building, and of course everyone knew everyone else's business. There was screaming and fighting heard regularly in the halls, but no other family could match the drama we dished out. An unwritten code existed in the building: no matter what was seen or heard, everyone stayed indoors and kept to themselves.

You can be sure that when we ran into the neighbors, the question, *"How is everything?"* was never asked. Instead, it was usually *"Sic fon may ah?"* (Have you eaten yet?) The polite response was, *"Sic bhow la"* (Ate plentifully).

Before I was even a year old, a fire began in the kitchen of the restaurant below. Smoke came billowing into our apartment late at night. My mother grabbed James and Dorothy while my father brought me and

May out. Mary was left in the apartment until one of the restaurant workers courageously ran in and carried her to safety. The flames were minimal but the smoke was potentially deadly.

At age four, I became ill with severe abdominal pains. My father didn't trust Western doctors and refused to seek help. By the time he carried me into the hospital, my appendix had burst and my body was stricken with peritonitis poisoning. The medical staff informed my parents that the prognosis was grim.

As I lay near death, I visualized my mother standing and crying in a room. I was able to describe the room and surgical equipment. We discovered later that the details were precise, except that she was down the hall in another area away from me.

I remember encountering a spirit and the beautiful, serene sensation that encompassed it. The spirit encouraged me to follow him, but I refused. He expressed concerns about the hardships that lay ahead in my life. I told him I couldn't bear to leave my mother. I would come to regret that decision. The horrors that I eventually faced throughout life later convinced me that the spirit was trying to save me from hell on earth.

Years later, during one of many close encounters with death I faced, it occurred to me that at age four, I only spoke Cantonese. So how did the spirit and I communicate? Evidently, it wasn't through conventional language.

Frank Choy, a bright, bold surgeon, was the physician on call. He performed an emergency appendectomy, miraculously saving my life. My stomach was pumped and tubes were inserted into my leg to draw the toxicity from my body. I spent a terrifying month in the hospital.

During recovery, my father again endangered my life. Still convinced that he could provide better treatment, he abducted me from the hospital. The result was a high fever and infection that sent me back to the intensive care unit. Dr. Choy was infuriated and threatened my father with criminal action.

"Are you trying to kill your son, Mr. Chin?!" If you continue jeopardizing his life, I'll bring you up on charges!"

My father reluctantly behaved himself.

It was discovered during my hospitalization that I had serious congenital heart defects. Major enlargement and a loud murmur indicated ventricle dysfunction. Of course, the doctors were shocked that it was overlooked at birth. I was referred to the Department of Cardiology at the University of California-San Francisco Medical Center.

Once a month, I was examined by their top cardiologists, all of whom were Caucasian. The doctors were the first non-Asian people I had encountered. It was terrifying for me to be touched and probed by strangers with bright-colored hair and eyes. I used to break free from my mother's hold and run down the hospital corridor screaming at the top of my lungs. I was also convinced the electrocardiogram pads placed on my chest would electrocute me. Surgery was put off until I was older and able to withstand the procedure.

My mother had to take time out for my appointments. She had a way of making sure I knew the burden my health problems placed on her. During the long bus rides to the medical center, she never said a word. My mother just sighed all the way, at times choosing to sit away from me. I felt bad for being so much trouble.

My mother's resentment of taking me to the doctors and hospitals may have been due in part to guilt. She shared with one of my sisters that she blamed herself more than my father for my health problems. She felt it was her responsibility to protect me during her pregnancy.

In the ensuing years, I required numerous hospitalizations and surgeries. My other siblings, however, enjoyed good health. The botched abortion attempt had long-term ramifications on my well-being and development.

A non-profit charitable organization took up my cause and covered all the medical expenses for my treatments. They dropped our case after my father falsified information, putting me at risk again with no medical coverage. They gave him ample opportunities to cooperate but he refused. My father stood his ground, insisting that he was more than capable of treating me; that I didn't need those doctors. Years later, as I was hemorrhaging from a collapsed lung, my father finally admitted his shortcomings.

My father was obsessed with treating his children with herbs. Our tiny kitchen often reeked of strong, exotic fumes from the medicine brewing on the stove. Our bowel movements were monitored and laxatives "loosely" prescribed.

My mother didn't exactly sit still for his medical antics. After my father pressured her into attempting to abort me, she second-guessed all his diagnoses and consulted her own internist. She accused my father of being a quack who purchased his diplomas. That went really well with him. All the kids in the family learned to be skilled mediators for our parents.

* * * *

My mother was emotionally unstable. Her fears were aggravated by my father's infidelity, which he denied, but was guilty of.

She attempted suicide on several occasions. Once we (the kids) had to break the bathroom door down and stop her as she began slashing her wrists. On several occasions, we had to restrain her from jumping out the window. I constantly worried that one day she might decide to take us out with her.

My mother had a hope chest that stored her prize possessions. From time to time, she showed off some of the beautiful sweaters she collected in her homeland. My sisters assumed that one day they'd have the privilege of wearing them.

One Friday afternoon, Mary came home to prepare for her eighth-grade graduation dance. None of us had anything resembling dress clothes, so Mary opened the hope chest. She put on one of Mommy's fancy sweaters.

"If Mommy was home, she'd say yea, huh?" Mary asked.

None of us responded. My mother was unpredictable in many ways. We all knew there was some risk involved.

Mary thought about running down to the sewing factory to get permission but there wasn't time. So off she went to the dance wearing the beautiful sweater.

We sat and crossed our fingers, praying that Mary would return first and put the sweater back without notice. Unfortunately, it didn't turn out that way. My mother came home and I held my breath.

I will never forget the look on my mother's face when Mary walked in wearing the sweater. It was as if the devil came through the door. My sister knew right away that she was in big trouble.

"Mommy, please don't be angry...I was wrong," she cried.

My mother charged toward Mary and yanked the sweater off. Mary started bawling. For the next few minutes, my mother screamed at the top of her lungs as my sister cried harder and harder. Finally my mother sat down. Her entire body was convulsing from anger. I just stood there, with my mouth open. The only sound was Mary weeping.

Without looking away from the table, my mother spoke up. I didn't recognize the voice; it was eerie.

"Bring me the scissors," she demanded.

"Mommy...Mommy...I'll never dare do this again. Go ahead and hit me," my sister pleaded through her tears.

I prayed that perhaps my mother was going to cut Mary's hair to punish her. But I knew it was going to be much worse. Mary begged and begged to be hit but my mother wasn't going to let her off that easily. At that point, I think each of us would have been willing to take a beating for Mary.

Finally, Mary brought the scissors to my mother. She carefully laid the material out and just like that, the beautiful sweater was sheared into pieces.

"Is there anything else you'd like to wear of mine?" she shouted.

I thought my mother was going to snip everything in the chest but she didn't. Her reaction toward Mary left me with the impression that although we were her children, she also perceived us as her enemies. She was a master at making us feel repulsive.

My mother was also paranoid, repeatedly warning us kids that one day our father would *"soct say ngor gay"* (kill us all). After a while, I kept a large knife under my mattress, not for fear of intruders, but to protect myself from my own family. In my mind, it was perfectly clear: the world is not a safe place.

By age eight, I was suffering from OCD (Obsessive Compulsive Disorder). I didn't know what it was or what to do. I washed my hands uncontrollably, often till they bled. I couldn't stand being touched, and everything had to be done in a specific order. I found myself counting the number of times my eyes blinked as well as the number of breaths I took. My dad and brother tormented me about it. I was also preoccupied with death. I was convinced I had a terminal illness and obsessed with the fear of my parents dying.

A small box containing baseball cards and a ping-pong ball was meticulously stored in a drawer. When all hell broke loose in the house, I went into my special box and rearranged it. I felt the only thing I had control of in the world was in that box.

* * * *

Violence was common in our home. It was easy to provoke my father after he got drunk, which occurred nightly. James, who is four years older, brutalized me for years. Perhaps he felt compelled to take on the role of man of the house and didn't know how to maintain control, resorting to constantly beating the "shit" out of my sister, May and me in order to rule his domain. Talk back or get in his way and I'd find myself with a bloody nose. My arms and legs were twisted to the brink of snapping. As I lay on the floor in tears, the savage would suddenly become a charmer, concerned about what he had done. James decided he should be forgiven. Because I reserved the right to stay angry, another beating was administered.

Dorothy never talked back and did whatever you asked. Mary was the eldest and James respected her. I was so distraught, I often thought of strangling or stabbing him while he slept. He finally left May alone when she dug her nail into his face during a scuffle, scarring him permanently. I witnessed it and felt a sense of redemption. He left me alone after I kicked him in the groin, but it wasn't enough for me. As we got older, my repressed anger still needed to be released on him. The years of abuse were far from being settled.

My father never beat the boys, but he sure took things out on my sisters. He would make a fist, then push the index and middle fingers out. With the knuckles of those fingers protruding, he would smash them against their heads. Chinese refer to the disciplinary blow as a *ling gawk.* In our house, my father frequently administered his ling gawks during dinner.

The seating arrangement at our makeshift dining table illustrated our family hierarchy. My father sat at one end and I was on the opposite side. Clockwise, my father was at the top of the table, followed by my mother, James, me, May and finally Dorothy. Mary was smart. She began working in her early teens and had an excuse for missing family meals.

My father was quiet when dinner started, but after a few drinks, he turned into a monster. Bottles of bourbon and whiskey were placed on the floor by his feet. We'd start giggling and he would demand silence. Outbursts continued with Dorothy receiving all the beatings. She sat on my father's right. Her head was in his direct line of fire. When she cried, it provoked him further. Often, Dorothy would arrive early and sit away from my father, but the seating order was dictated by him and not to be questioned.

I could usually tell when he was about to "go off." Not only would he give you the evil eye, but his jaw muscles would also pulsate rapidly. I tried warning my sisters, but they never saw it coming. Dorothy got hit once for staring at my father's jaw.

Eventually, the rest of us boycotted the table and left my father eating alone. We scurried when he got up from the table. Once he slept it off for about half-an-hour, he was mellow again. Then he couldn't wait to get out of the house.

* * * *

My father always dashed out after dinner. So I followed him out the door and tagged along wherever he went. As a child, I relished those times together, as they provided an opportunity for me to bond with him. For better or worse, I longed to be with him.

He was quite involved in Chinatown politics and an active member in the Kuomintang Nationalist Party. There were a lot of boring meetings. Yet, my eyes would light up when he spoke. No matter how abusive my father was toward me, I still idolized him.

The KMT sponsored a Chinese language school in its headquarters, and my father taught there part-time. It was just a block from our house. In time, he was elected principal of the school. This is one of the most prestigious positions to hold in the KMT and the community. Education has always been highly valued in our culture, so teachers, especially principals, are held in the highest regard.

Although my father repeatedly swore to my mother that he was broke, he always seemed to have money for gambling and drinking. We spent most nights in mah-jong parlors—not the most conducive environment for a small child, with their scrappy furniture, smoke-filled rooms, ivory tiles clanging and players screaming profanities at one another. *"Dill nay ga lo mo"* (Fuck your mother) and *"kai dai"* (bastard) were hurled across the tables. I usually slept on the couch or floor until the wee hours. I anticipated arguments when my mother accompanied my father. One or both would lose and take it out on the other.

After I started kindergarten, it was just my father and me at the nightly mah-jong games. I had to keep an eye out for him since he'd be in a stupor from the alcohol as we walked through Chinatown after dinner. When he fell, there wasn't much I could do.

"Daddy, hey sun" (get up), I pleaded, while yanking on his arm. It was quite embarrassing as he was a well-known figure in the community. People stopped and offered to help. I could tell they felt sorry for me. They were often more concerned about me than my father.

My father allocated time between dinner and mah-jong for my Tai Chi lessons. I wanted to study karate at the YMCA, but my father insisted on teaching me martial arts himself. The lingering effects of the alcohol on him made the effort quite frustrating. We used the assembly hall in KMT headquarters, which was filled with photographs of Sun Yat Sen, Chiang Kai Shek, and other forefathers of the Republic of China. An elderly janitor was usually there, cleaning up.

It was quite hilarious if you can picture the two of us in identical poses with our arms extended and legs bent, staring at each other. We would be stuck because "Master Daddy" couldn't remember the next sequence of moves. I was forbidden to question his instruction and struggled not to laugh. Eventually, the janitor initiated a ritual of practicing Tai Chi next to us. I had to sneak a peek at him in order to rescue my father from our predicament. That old janitor must have had many a good laugh on us.

* * * *

"Ah Chell, jow-la" (Son, it's time to go), my father would say, waking me up when the mah-jong game ended. As we walked home, I could tell by the way he held my hand if he had won or lost. When he won, I received a percentage of the winnings, so we were essentially gambling partners. Our ritual was to pick up *sil-yeh* (late-night snack) at Sam Wo's on the way home. When my father lost, the walk seemed a lot longer. I went straight to bed and left him sitting alone, which he preferred.

My father was not exactly the best role model. My mother taught us to do the right thing, while my father was extremely dishonest. He lived by his own rules. He bullied people and believed in screwing the other guy first. Basically, my father lived on the dark side.

One day at a hardware store in Chinatown, I followed and watched him stroll from aisle to aisle, where he stuffed a measuring tape, paintbrushes and putty knives in his coat pockets. My father walked up to the counter and paid for a piece of sandpaper. Everything was sticking out of his pockets. He had total disregard for his crime, and the proprietor didn't dare confront him. Of course I had to promise not to tell my mother. We had an understanding that my mother was never to be told anything.

* * * *

I had my first job even before starting kindergarten shining shoes for ten cents. My brother and I ventured to Saint Mary's Square Park in Chinatown and worked afternoons and weekends, shining shoes till dark. On good days, businessmen handed us quarters in appreciation of our efforts.

Unfortunately, we also had to be wary of men in the park trying to lure us with money to satisfy their sick urges. We didn't know what pedophiles were back then, only that these men, who approached us with devious stares, had to be avoided and dealt with. They were labeled *Hom Sup Low* (Dirty Old Men). At times, we turned to older street kids for assistance. We baited the weirdoes into an alley and beat the shit out of 'em. They were robbed for good measure. This was never reported, not even to our parents. I accepted early on that there were bad people and lots of secrets in Chinatown. One learns quickly about survival on the streets.

Categorizing us as latchkey kids would be an understatement. Lacking supervision and a sense of right or wrong, we passed our time stealing, fighting and gambling. We climbed rooftops, scaled elevator shafts and played cat-and-mouse with the police. Most of the activities involved high-risk behavior that we carried into our teens and adulthood.

* * * *

With barely enough money to keep food on the table, my mother insisted that we attend Saint Mary's Catholic School, half a block from our home. The tuition alone was nearly half of what my mother earned at the garment factory. She wasn't religious but wanted us to learn good values. My mother was also concerned about a busy intersection we'd have to cross in order to attend the public school, so the parochial school being just a few doors down the street provided her with peace of mind.

I do not have fond memories of grammar school. Because Chinese was my only language at the time, I struggled in school from the start. Placed with the lowest academic group in classes, I was labeled stupid. The aptitude tests in English were foreign to me. Most of my classmates were third-generation Chinese-Americans and didn't understand my difficulties. Of course, most of them were monolingual. The only Chinese they knew was *Gung Hay Fat Choy,* which got them "lucky money" for New Year's. I was already fluent in three dialects of Chinese by the time I enrolled in school.

In our home, we spoke *Sam Yup* (Cantonese) and *Sze Yup* (Toishan dialect). I picked up the third dialect,

Lhong Dhown, from friends at the playground.

As a young child, I also suffered from an eating disorder. I disliked most food and was fixated on rice and peanuts. Night after night, that's all I ate. During lunch at Saint Mary's, which was served in a basement auditorium, we were required to clean off our plates. Initially forced to eat, which caused me to vomit, I finally refused. My punishment was loss of recess privileges. Student-hostesses assigned to my table resented me, as I caused each of them demerits.

Jason Fung and Frank Lau were my best friends. Both were recent immigrants from Hong Kong. Frank was the strong, gutsy one; Jason was tall and shy; I was known as the conniving one. We spoke Cantonese among ourselves and did everything together. We even went to the bathroom together. The three of us would stand around the commode and pee at the same time, crisscrossing our streams. We didn't have any hang-ups about silly things like that.

All of us came from troubled homes and endured

similar pains. I shared secrets with them that I never trusted anyone else with. We discussed fears about our homes and lives; whether God approved of us. We talked seriously about running away together. We were only in second grade. Who could have guessed all of us would end up in gangs, and one of us would be convicted of murder.

I got into fights almost daily. Sometimes, it seemed as though I spent more time in Principal Sister Mildred's office, getting paddled, than in class. A pale-skinned, tiny woman with folds of wrinkle hanging out of her habit, she grind her teeth and grunted as she delivered each blow. Initially, her rage shocked me. Soon, I accepted her as disturbed, just like me. I knew that it was only a matter of time before I grabbed the paddle and turned it on her.

The worst time for me in school was during Open House. We were required to sit at our desks whether our parents attended or not. My father and mother never participated in school activities. I think my oldest sister Mary and I took it the hardest. It was torture for me to sit up straight with my hands neatly clasped on the desk, with my tests and class assignments neatly piled on the top right corner. I'd stare at the door and prayed that my parents would show up—they never did. They were usually the only parents missing. There was a lot of resentment acted out the next day in the schoolyard. I attacked anyone who teased me about my parents' absence.

I attended St. Mary's for eight years, including two years in the third grade. My brother and I were out of control, and they held us back together. We broke all their records for truancy, fighting and stealing. Corporal punishment didn't deter us. The most difficult transition I faced in staying behind my class was the friendships. I gradually became distant from Jason and Frank. New friendships had to be established with kids who were a year younger. I never really clicked with anyone except a kid named Winston.

After I completed the sixth grade, my parents gave in to my pleas, allowing me to transfer to public school. In private, Sister Mildred made it clear to me that I was not welcomed back the following year. That suited me fine. I couldn't wait to get out of there. I swore to go after that "old penguin." She treated me like I was possessed by the devil. When I left St. Mary's, I abandoned my belief in God and religion as well.

Excerpt from Born to Lose: Memoirs of a Compulsive Gambler

©2005 by Hazelden Foundation

Chapter 1.

Home Group

I could barely keep my eyes open as I gently shook the tiny hand bell at 8:03 P.M. to officially start the meeting. I had just returned home to San Francisco from a business trip, catching back-to-back "red-eye" flights, and debriefing my client in Silicon Valley for most of the day. The rain outside was coming down in buckets, with pellets of hail crashing against the church's ornate windows. As members continued trampling in with their umbrellas and raincoats dripping on the carpet, I shook my head, recalling that we recently paid the pastor to have it professionally cleaned. I rang the bell a little louder to tone down the laughter coming from the back of the room. Something in my gut told me that—for better or for worse—this was not going to be a dull meeting. After all, this was my home group.

The small, yellow "combo" books that serve as the cornerstone of our recovery program were neatly laid out in front of each chair on the long conference table, and the strong aroma of coffee from the kitchen filled the air of the warm, dimly lit library. In spite of the winter storm, it looked as though we were going to have a full house. So far, I counted twenty-two heads. We would have to bring in more chairs.

As secretary of the San Francisco Friday night Gamblers Anonymous (GA) meeting, I jot down each person's first name and last initial in our official notebook as they enter the room. Our profile is more or less representative of a GA group in a culturally rich metropolitan area. On this particular evening, we had eighteen Caucasians (as far as I could tell); two Asians; one Latino; and one African American. There were nineteen males and three females. The youngest member looked to be in his mid-twenties, and the oldest had just turned seventy-eight. Among gambling addicts, men outnumber women approximately five to one. Also, women tend to be closet gamblers, start gambling later in life, and have a higher incidence of dual addictions. Only two to four percent of the women in GA attend meetings regularly, so my home group's above average female membership is something I am truly proud of.

You'd never know it, but this group of unassuming-looking citizens is made up of some pretty colorful characters. Three have been convicted of felony embezzlement, one for larceny, another for armed robbery, and more than three-quarters have committed or considered committing various crimes—all to feed their gambling addiction. Everyone present has bounced a check, faced bankruptcy, and at least contemplated suicide. More than half are recovering from multiple addictions. A few proclaim that gambling is harder to kick than heroin and crack; they don't hesitate to provide vivid details. Two are homeless and another three are mandated by court to attend. One guy is out on a pass from county jail and will be returning there at the end of the meeting. Within six months, three members will no longer be with us. They will all die of sudden causes—one within forty-eight hours after relapsing in Reno. Profound statements made by each of them at tonight's meeting would resonate deep within me for years to come.

Downstairs, a Gam-Anon meeting is taking place, where several wives, a mother, and a live-in girlfriend of problem gamblers use the Twelve Step recovery program to learn about compulsive gambling, to heal, and to offer support to one another. All of these women share a common bond: At one time or another, their lives had been devastated because someone they loved lost himself in gambling. When compulsive gamblers hit bottom, their spouses often suffer just as much or even more, since many were in the dark about the addiction and are suddenly forced to face it head on when the secret is uncovered. As the responsible party in the marriage, they're left to hold the family together, financially as well as emotionally.

Gam-Anon members sometimes envy spouses of addicts in other fellowships whose drug of choice is alcohol, food, or sex. At least with those addictions, the healing can begin as soon as the addiction is in remission, whereas in gambling, the financial damage can last a lifetime and beyond. It doesn't come as a surprise that one of the wives in this group had attempted suicide, since spouses of compulsive gamblers are three times more likely to commit suicide than the general population. Fortunately, this particular wife survived and through Gam-Anon learned that her husband's addiction isn't her fault. In fact, she now serves as the group's secretary, sharing her wisdom with others who are living with a compulsive gambler. She has become adept at recognizing co-dependent relationships and encourages spouses to stop enabling their addictive partners.

Back at my meeting, a new face was sitting to my right, fidgeting in her chair: a blonde woman who appeared to be in her early forties. She reminded me of my college math professor—except that the person sitting here looked like someone who was in deep mourning. I sensed tremendous pain in her voice when she called earlier in the week to confirm the meeting time and to get directions. Her name was Rita, and she was awaiting sentencing for forging company checks, to the tune of over $150,000. Like myself, she had a weakness for blackjack. A gentleman also called yesterday and indicated that he would be attending, but he hadn't shown up yet. I glanced at the door every five minutes or so but knew that getting to that first meeting is difficult for most compulsive gamblers. It certainly was for me.

Just before 9 P.M., we begin the therapy portion of the meeting, where a number of us take turns sharing our stories with Rita. I must have heard each member's gambling history at least a dozen times, and the details do get old, but there's nothing like watching newcomers' eyes light up when they identify with someone's share. You can never predict who the new member will connect with. I've been around long enough to know that it's not based on race, gender, religion, or socio-economic status. If anything, within the fellowship, opposites seem to attract. Rita is about to discover that she shares many attributes with GA members. Specifically, some of us are highly proficient with tabulating numbers and have a knack for attention to minute details. In theory, this gives us an advantage when we're gambling, whether it's counting cards in blackjack, analyzing the horses and conditions at the racetrack, studying financial reports of public companies in the stock market, maintaining players' performances for sports betting, or even monitoring the letters and numbers in bingo.

Unfortunately, our addiction overrides our skills, leaving us with a false sense of superiority.

In GA (as well as other Twelve Step programs), we believe that when new members are present, they are the most important people in the room. Most problem gamblers hit rock bottom just prior to joining us for the first time. More often than not, they're consumed with guilt and hopelessness. They have run out of lies and exhausted their resources, both legal and illegal. There's no more long shot or dream world. Their low self-esteem has been validated, and they feel worthless. All the negative messages they have internalized since childhood are magnified. Their self-destructive tendencies have reached a climax. They are consumed with shame and self-hatred. Their fresh wounds remind us how insidious the disease can be. The newcomer is like a ghost from our past, making sure we don't forget how susceptible we are to our urges. The new member also offers each of us an opportunity to reach out and practice Step Twelve, which is to carry the GA message to other compulsive gamblers, both in and outside of the fellowship. Reaching out to others is a powerful tool. Our recovery depends on it.

And finally, we want to make newcomers feel as

welcome as possible, because the road to recovery usually consists of a lot of bumps and detours. If they don't return next week, or slip down the line and return to gambling, it's important for them to know that the GA door is always open. The best way for us to ensure this is to preserve their anonymity, while maintaining a safe, non-judgmental environment where they can share their pain and receive support.

As Roger C., our resident sports handicapper, slouched forward and recounted in his baritone voice, for the umpteenth time, how he made his first bet in high school picking the Oakland Raiders over the Philadelphia Eagles in Super Bowl XV, two members sitting directly across from one another were making funny faces and lobbing candy wrappers at each other. I tapped on the table with my knuckles to halt their juvenile behavior, which is all too common whenever you have a gathering of compulsive gamblers. Many began their addictions in their teens (much earlier in my case), which also stalled their emotional maturity. The inability to accept responsibility and to deal with everyday life issues are major obstacles for compulsive gamblers in recovery.

As we approached 10:00 P.M., I announced that we had time for one last speaker. At that point, about half of the members had given therapy. As I searched the room for a volunteer, Dennis T., our treasurer, raised his hand.

"Go ahead, Dennis."

"Well, actually, I was hoping that you would share last. I think it would be helpful for Rita."

Dennis caught me off guard, as I hadn't planned on speaking. Glancing over at Rita, she cocked her head slightly and raised her eyebrows. Our newcomer had nonverbally seconded the motion. Suddenly, I felt a burst of energy shooting through my body. I sat up and took a deep breath.

"Okay…my name is Bill L., and I'm a recovering compulsive gambler."

"Hi Bill!" the group shouted in unison.

"My history of gambling really began before I was born…"

Made in the USA
Middletown, DE
03 July 2016